Witchcraft and Magic in Europe
Volume 1. Biblical and Pagan Societies

THE ATHLONE HISTORY OF WITCHCRAFT AND MAGIC IN EUROPE

Series Editors
Bengt Ankarloo (University of Lund)
Stuart Clark (University of Swansea)

The roots of European witchcraft and magic lie in Hebrew and other ancient Near Eastern cultures and in the Celtic, Nordic, and Germanic traditions of the continent. For two millennia, European folklore and ritual have been imbued with the belief in the supernatural, yielding a rich trove of histories and images.

Witchcraft and Magic in Europe combines traditional approaches of political, legal, and social historians with a critical synthesis of cultural anthropology, historical psychology, and gender studies. The series provides a modern, scholarly survey of the supernatural beliefs of Europeans from ancient times to the present day. Each volume of this ambitious series contains the work of distinguished scholars chosen for their expertise in a particular era or region.

Witchcraft and Magic in Europe
Biblical and Pagan Societies

FREDERICK H. CRYER
MARIE-LOUISE THOMSEN

THE ATHLONE PRESS
LONDON

First published in 2001 by
THE ATHLONE PRESS
A Continuum imprint
The Tower Building, 11 York Road, London SE1 7NX

© The Contributors 2001

British Library Cataloguing in Publication Data
A catalogue record for this book is available
from the British Library

ISBN 0 485 89001 1 HB
0 485 89101 8 PB

Typeset by Centraserve, Saffron Walden, Essex
Printed and bound in Great Britain by
Bookcraft (Bath) Ltd

Contents

Illustrations

General Introduction

Obviously, European magic beliefs and actions as we meet them in the historical sources of medieval and modern times have a long prehistory. To trace that prehistory is a complex enterprise. The interpretation of the archaeological evidence from all over Europe could give us indications about the endogenous elements of a cosmology among our ancestors. Attention to the cultural effects of prehistorical migrations across the Eurasian continent including the impact of the Indo-Aryan diffusion would be another crucial part of such a genealogical inquiry. The role of learned specialist ideas transmitted in written sources as opposed to the oral tradition of the common people and, as a related problem, the possible differentiation of belief systems connected with class distinctions, would have to be assessed. The field is virtually open since all history has a prehistory without bounds. In the end the historian himself has to decide where to begin and in so doing give the reasons for his decision.

The Athlone History of Witchcraft and Magic in Europe starts with two companion volumes serving as a backdrop to the European drama. This first volume deals with the cultures of the Ancient Near East, the second with the ancient cultures of the Mediterranean basin, the Greeks and the Romans. All these widely different cultural streams eventually converge in the history of Western Europe from early medieval times. They all in common include written sources and are therefore part of a literate tradition which became universalized in the learned institutions of the West. This in turn makes them accessible to investigation with the use of historical methods. So here is, in our view, where the history of European magic should begin.

From Mesopotamia we have numerous cuneiform inscriptions

on monuments and clay tablets. As a result Sumerian and Akkadian magic is documented by a large amount of incantations and instructions for rituals. The Old Testament contains a plethora of references to magic beliefs and practices in old Palestine. A revised interpretation of these sources in the light of recent archaeological and historical information and with the use of comparative cultural anthropology is now emerging.

In trying to outline the history of magic we are immediately confronted with the problem of classification. How can we define magic as opposed to other beliefs and actions? The easiest way out would be to resort to the everyday connotation of it as ignorant superstition or to its normative classification as a particular kind of prohibited activity. In doing so we would hardly be able to step outside the delimitations of our own immediate conscience and that would prevent us from reaching a genuine understanding both of the historical function of magic and its place in the field of human actions. But even with a theoretically more open definition we are faced with numerous difficulties. After all, what beliefs and practices are to be classified as magical? On what grounds do we regard certain sources as belonging to the magical sphere as opposed to geographical or botanical knowledge? In fact most of these classifications are made from the vantage point of view of rival cosmologies, including our own. As Marie-Louise Thomsen points out, much of the 'magic' formulas encountered in the Mesopotamian clay tablets have been labelled as such by modern Assyrologists. They constitute a more or less residual category in the close vicinity of both 'religion' and 'medicine'. By the Assyrians themselves these activities and beliefs were regarded neither as forbidden nor superstitious and ineffective. On the contrary: they were part of a generally accepted code of behaviour, reasonable precautions against the ubiquitous perils in a world where gods and demons still walked among men. Such measures might even require considerable skill.

It is difficult for us to relax our rational scepticism in the face of beliefs so blatantly in opposition to what we know about how things work. Consider the role of water in ritual purification. Although we are willing to admit this as a 'symbolic' analogy based on the practice of washing in water, we are reluctant to regard the ritual as 'real' in the same sense as the physical cleaning process of taking a shower. And this is precisely where we take issue with the Assyrians. To them the 'ritual' performance was as real and effective as the morning ritual is to us.

The concept of magic has played an important role as an element in the evolutionary theory of religions. There it was placed in the early, 'primitive' stages, before the rise of religion proper. Monotheism was seen as the latest and highest form of religion and Israel its first historical realization. As a consequence, magic in the world of the Old Testament had to be explained away as an exogenous, alien aberration. But, in fact, magic is central not only in 'primitive' societies but in 'high cultural' civilizations as well, in ancient India, China and the Near East. The strict separation of magic and religion is not possible to uphold. It appears to be the product of a particular western historical experience finding its expression in nineteenth century evolutionary historicism. Frederick Cryer's essay in this volume demonstrates how closely magic is associated with religious practice and political struggle in ancient Palestine. Stressing the 'embeddedness' of magic Cryer challenges the traditional interpretations of magic in the Bible, which regard it as a foreign intrusion into what has been held to be the first monotheistic society.

Mainstream European cosmology has been dualistic at least since the days of Descartes. It means that we make a strict distinction between things material and spiritual. Most other civilizations are not dualistic in this cartesian sense. The idea that immaterial spirits can influence, harm or heal the bodies of men and beasts comes naturally to them, as it did to our own ancestors. Our modern Western insistense on finding a coherent causality within the physical world, an attitude we call natural science, would be alien to people in other times or places. In a unified universe with a holistic causality our separation of physical from spiritual categories has no meaning.

This does not necessarily mean that one cosmology seen as a cognitive system is as good as any other and that we subscribe to a radically anarchic epistemology when we relativize the concept of truth as we encounter it in historic times and in other cultures. But in order to do justice to and really understand the past we must try to read the sources it has left to us with hermeneutic imagination and generous empathy. No more, no less. The reader is cautioned to accept the term magic not as a patronizing and pejorative label on certain modes of thought in the past or somewhere else in the contemporary world, but as a descriptive category of strategies aimed at influencing the powers not immediately accessible with ordinary physical means.

There are more difficulties. To call an action magic is to place it outside established practice. Often the purpose is to stigmatize it. But not always. Magic may be desired or resorted to for a number of reasons. But to achieve its particular distinction, magic must be in some way unusual, spectacular even miraculous. Precisely for that reason we must also be cautious not to exoticize it. Such a tendency is inherent in the numerous stories about magic both in the Bible and in other ancient texts. The narrative propagation of magic beliefs and the dramatic staging of magical practices underline their amazing or horrifying aspects. Stories told about the great magicians tend to enhance the romance and wonder associated with their trade. In contrast, actual magical practice as empirically observed is often rather prosaic. But folk stories about magic provide an important imaginary framework which permits a given situation to be redefined as an example of magical healing, cursing or counter-magic. The need of novelty is part of these dramatic requirements. A spell or a curse when used over and over again will lose its power and has to be replaced by something new and more powerful. A society where magic is prevalent is always open to borrowing new procedures from other societies, as it is always the next spell or ritual that is potentially the most effective. This observation may help to explain the heavy dependece on orientalism of our Western magical lore from Madame Blavatsky to the New Age.

Magic when coolly observed as an object of scholarly research takes on a different character than magic as living practice and experience. The problem of combining a dispassionate scientific study with the hermeneutic empathy of a historicist approach is particularly acute in the case of belief systems that are far removed from the experience of the observer. You cannot live in the house at the same time as you observe it as a piece of architecture. To be inside is, to some extent, to be unaware of the exterior, and vice versa.

A decidedly constructivist position would be to assert that magic when observed in the historical sources exists only in the eye of the beholder; is nothing but an idea in the head of the historian at his desk in the library. Most of us would probably be reluctant to go that far. We would at least assign to magic some sort of independent reality, even though the precise concept of magic might be a late terminological invention. People in the past, we think, have acted in a number of ways that we in the present find convenient to lump together as one coherent category, magic. We may even concede that the historical actors themselves, reflecting on their own behaviour, probably would be unable to make any clear distinctions between magic and ordinary rational actions. Admitting this, we often talk about magic as being 'embedded' in a culture, so deeply immersed under the skin as to be 'the most natural thing in the world', and therefore invisible.

So, under the treatment of modern scholarship magic is twice removed from its erstwhile position as a historically authentic category: first by the scientific criticism of the *Lumières*, reducing it to a non-rational and physically ineffectual procedure among primitive and ignorant savages; secondly by postmodern deconstruction, depriving it even of its place in the minds of the magical operators. Magic, our object of study, threatens to disappear altogether before our eyes. But if we accept on the one hand that our investigation of the world of magic is a backward projection of its place in our contemporary taxonomy; and if we look on the other hand at past magic not only as a stage in the progression towards the present but as a category in its own right; then we may be able to combine our sceptical self-reflection with a methodology that accepts the past as a past reality.

A number of important themes emerge from the essays in this volume. The social and in a broad sense political foundations of magic are visible in the struggle for precedence among cults and ritual practices. To be able to monopolize divination is to wield power in a more general sense. Among the Jews in ancient Palestine magic finds its place within a system of petty kingdoms competing for power by developing ritual practices, and by condemning as heretic those of nearby cults. The famous and often quoted ban on magic and sorcery in the Old Testament can be interpreted not as a general prohibition, but as a stigmatization of usages among adjacent ritual groups. But magic is visible not only in the struggle for power among kings and tribal elites but also, and perhaps in particular, in the daily life of ordinary people. It reflects the numerous situations where passions and desires drive men to action. Among many other strategies of love and hate they resort to magical procedures. Where population density is high enough to create a market, specialized operators, magicians, compete in offering their services and an esoteric tradition is gradually established. We have no difficulties in recognizing the basic and perennial social drama underlying these efforts to control the forces of life. Under the veil of strange ritual and ceremonial practices, incantations and spells, we can identify ordinary conflicts, fears and everyday concerns about social esteem. In the end this recognition of existential human needs is the very foundation of our interest in people of the past, however irrational and alien they may seem to us at first. Sometimes the formal pattern of magic, the styles of action and invocations, appears to be so stable as to look almost archetypal. The water ordeal of Mesopotamia is a reversed mirror of that in Europe during the great sixteenth century witch hunt. The practice of injuring a doll in the shape of your enemy is prevalent over thousands of years. The significance and power of words both spoken and written is recognized both in Babylon and in medieval Europe.

As we proceed in the following volumes of this series to classical Greece and Rome and further to medieval and early modern Europe, we will recognize many of these elements of belief and action as belonging to the *longue durée*, to our perennial mentalities, and that, consequently, the studies in this volume of magic in the ancient Near East were relevant for our task.

Bengt Ankarloo
Stuart Clark

PART 1

Witchcraft and Magic in Ancient Mesopotamia

Marie-Louise Thomsen

INTRODUCTION

Mesopotamia: the Land, its People and History

In Antiquity, the land between Euphrates and Tigris, with the classical Greek name of Mesopotamia (today approximately Iraq), was for a very long period a powerful state with an enormous influence, not only in political affairs but also in the areas of science, technology, literature and religion. Its legacy can still be traced even in our modern Western European civilization. Two main streams of information about Mesopotamia were available to Europeans in post-Antiquity: the Bible and various classical authors. These sources concentrated on outstanding achievements like the cities of Babylon and Nineveh and the Tower of Babel, or on various historical or legendary personalities, for instance Nebuchadnezzar and Belshazzar or Nimrod and Semiramis. The Chaldeans, a people of the southern part of Mesopotamia, were also mentioned for their proficiency in the fields of astronomy and divination.

From the middle of the nineteenth century this picture of the ancient civilizations of Assyria and Babylonia was supplemented by original sources: monumental inscriptions, works of art and, not least, thousands of clay tablets were excavated. Through this new material the older tradition was confirmed on many points, but contradictory information, on the other hand, caused a crisis in the understanding of the Bible as a divine revelation. Today the history of Mesopotamia is written on the basis of a great variety of original sources: historical inscriptions, chronicles and annals, and administrative and juridical documents, as well as literary texts like myths, epics, fables, proverbs, hymns, lamentations and even humorous and satirical compositions. The field of witchcraft and magic, in particular, is documented by a large amount of incantations and instructions for rituals, providing much valuable information about this aspect of ancient life.

Earliest History and First Settlements

Whereas remains of human settlements in the surrounding areas are attested as early as 8500 BC, the alluvial plain was inhabited much later. This is due to the hot and dry climate which at times makes grazing as well as farming impossible. Not until the population had become sufficiently well organized to create an intensive irrigation agriculture could more extensive settlements arise. It was a long process finally resulting in the development of urban life, civilization and writing at the end of the fourth millennium BC. Construction and maintenance of an irrigation system implies a certain degree of organization and political leadership but once this is established the reward is abundant yields and even a surplus of food, which is itself the basis for expanding, and exchanging goods with neighbouring societies. On the other hand, the system is vulnerable to any irregularity; negligence caused by warlike encounters or other disorganization of the society may generate a breakdown of the water supply and, at worst, results in famine and the devastation of large areas.

The flourishing farming societies and growing cities along the rivers tempted nomadic tribes and hunting peoples both from the mountains in the East and from the West to progress along the banks of Euphrates. Cultivating the alluvial plain was, therefore, not the task of a single 'nation', but rather the result of this rendezvous of many groups with various origins and different conditions of life. Sometimes foreigners were peacefully absorbed and left only a few traces of their own language and culture, but more than once the fall of the ruling dynasty was caused by an attack by newcomers. Above all, two peoples dominated the culture and intellectual life of Mesopotamia: the Sumerians, possibly among the first inhabitants of the alluvial plain, and the

Akkadians, a people speaking a Semitic language and later known as the Babylonians in the south and the Assyrians in the north.

The Sumerian City-States

Southern Mesopotamia was organized into several city-states consisting of a major city and the surrounding land with some minor settlements or villages. The sanctuary of the city-god, the main protector of the inhabitants and closely connected with the special conditions of life in the community, was an important institution, and the head of a city-state was both a secular leader and the priest of the city-god. Already at the end of the fourth millennium a primitive kind of writing was invented as an aid for the administration of the land and the workers of the city-states, emerging first in the temple of Uruk and from here spreading to other cities. The oldest written records were accounts and lists of income and expenses, using pictures and symbols for goods, animals and numbers. Gradually writing became a medium for recording both prose and poetry, but for this the scribes had to develop a new syllabary of both signs for verbs and signs with phonetic values for grammatical elements. Only at this stage, *c.* 2900 BC, can it be said with certainty that the language of the texts is Sumerian, and the culture of the early civilization has therefore been claimed as Sumerian. However, despite lengthy debate, no final agreement or definite solutions have been reached concerning the date when this people settled in southern Mesopotamia or the degree to which they shared the work of cultivation with other ethnic groups.

The Akkadians: Babylonians and Assyrians

Whereas the Sumerians established their cities in the southern part of the alluvial plain, a people speaking a Semitic language and later known as the Akkadians settled themselves in the northern areas around the ancient town of Kish. Sumerians and Akkadians lived side by side for a very long period, mutually influencing each other in many fields: language, religion, social structures, etc. The cultural interaction and bilateral exchange were of such an extent that, in many cases, it does not make sense to try to differentiate Sumerian from Akkadian culture.

During the second half of the third millennium competition between the city-states intensified, each seeking to dominate the others as much as possible, until at last the land was united under one leader, a Semite with the throne name Šarru-kēn (Biblical form: Sargon), a legendary person in Mesopotamian history. The residence, Akkade, which he founded gave the name to his people – the Akkadians. From now on Akkadian language played a more important role and in the following centuries it superseded Sumerian as the everyday language even in the south.

Then, the political situation in Mesopotamia changed again, the dynasty of Akkade fell, and the city-states flourished anew. From now on several individual cities tried to take over the leadership of the land, and finally Hammurapi (1792–1750), the king of a hitherto almost unknown city, Babylon, succeeded in controlling not only the southern parts of Mesopotamia, the land that we today call Babylonia, but also neighbouring areas along the Euphrates.

In the north, Akkadians had already been settled for a long period, but about this population and its rulers there is much less written information. The name of the main god of this area was Aššur (or Assur) which was also the name of the capital. At the time when Hammurapi and his successors ruled Babylonia, the kings of Aššur controlled the northern parts of Mesopotamia and important trading routes went from Aššur to Anatolia where Assyrian merchants did business, primarily in tin and textiles. The Assyrians were not as strongly influenced by the Sumerian culture as their neighbours in the south but they admired the highly developed civilization of Babylonia and adopted its customs as well as its literature and learned tradition.

The empire of Hammurapi and his successors lasted only until 1594 BC when the fall of the Old Babylonian dynasty was caused by an attack by the Hittite army which Babylonia, weakened at that time, could not resist. For the next two hundred years written sources from Mesopotamia are scarce and after this gap several changes in the conditions of power are obvious. The Kassites, coming from the eastern region along the river Diyala, obtained rulership of Babylonia, Hittites established their empire in Asia Minor, and Hurrians were settled in the area north of Assyria. For some time Assyria had presumably been a vassal of the Mitanni kingdom in Syria (centering along the Habur river), but with the Hittite victory over Mitanni in the fourteenth century BC Assyria was again free to act as an independent state. In this period Mesopotamian contacts with Egypt and the western states were intensified and the fourteenth and thirteenth centuries were truly an age of international relations. Although Mesopotamia did not exercise military supremacy beyond its borders, the intellectual influence was important, with Babylonian as the international language of this period and the Hittites as well as the Hurrians using cuneiform for writing their own languages. As a result of the widespread use of cuneiform and the Babylonian language, other Near Eastern countries became acquainted with Babylonian literature and science as well.

Under the Kassite dynasty Babylonia prospered from political stability and wealth, the latter due especially to international trade routes passing through the land. Articles exported from Mesopotamia, such as textiles and horses, were exchanged for precious metals and luxury goods; Egypt for instance sent ebony, ivory and, most important, gold, which became the economic standard during this period.

The First Millennium: The Neo-Assyrian Empire

The military power of Assyria gradually increased and the kings led countless campaigns, either defending the borders to the north and east against the mountain peoples or expanding westwards attempting to control Syria and even the rich cities along the coast of the Mediterranean Sea. Although the Assyrian army was powerful and the campaigns often successful, it was difficult to retain the supremacy over the conquered land and it seems as if every king had to reconquer the territories captured by his predecessor. The real days of glory began for the Assyrian empire in the eighth century BC with Tiglath-Pileser III (744–727) who defeated the northern kingdom Urartu and thus alone controlled the whole of Syria.

With its southern neighbour, Babylonia, Assyria had a special relationship. The Assyrians admired and respected the Babylonian culture and were in many ways influenced by its customs, religion and literature; they even used the Babylonian language in inscriptions and official documents. However, the Assyrian king could not tolerate a strong and independent, and perhaps even hostile, ruler in the south, since the political and economic interests of both states were practically identical. Although the Assyrian kings probably did not really want to subdue Babylonia and make it a province of their empire, they sought to control the political situation in the south. In the last centuries of the second millennium the history of Mesopotamia is characterized by a trial of strength between its two countries, mostly with Assyria as the superior. Under the Neo-Assyrian kings, from the beginning of the first millennium BC, rebellions were repeatedly initiated by the Chaldeans, originally a western Semitic nomadic tribe, now living in the extreme south on the shores of the Persian Gulf, and these at last brought about the destruction of Babylon by Sennacherib in 689 BC. The next king, Esarhaddon (680–669), was pro-Babylonian and restored Babylon, also making one of his sons, Šamaš-šum-ukin, king of Babylon, whereas a younger son, Assurbanipal, became king of Assyria (668–627). Esarhaddon too was a successful conqueror; he brought Egypt and the Medes under his dominance, but Egypt was lost again under Assurbanipal and the Medes remained a threat to the Assyrian empire. Assurbanipal also had to suppress a Babylonian rebellion led by his brother Šamaš-šum-ukin.

Only with the decline of Assyria caused by the Medes and sealed by the fall of Nineveh in 612 BC, did the king of Babylon, Nabopolassar (629–605), a Chaldean, succeed in gaining independence, even acting as the heir of the Assyrian empire. His son and successor, Nebuchadnezzar II (604–562), known for the conquest of Jerusalem in 586 BC, rebuilt Babylon to be one of the seven wonders of the world in Antiquity. Nebuchadnezzar also tried to conquer Egypt but was defeated, and under his successors the Babylonian power gradually declined. In 555 BC a most controversial person, Nabonidus, came to the throne. He was not of royal family; his mother was a priestess of the moon god in Harran, and his father was unknown. Nabonidus's loyalty to the moon god brought him into opposition with the priests of Marduk in Babylon and this situation, as well as other political decisions, made the king disliked among the population. In contemporary texts Nabonidus is accused of blasphemy and madness, and when at last Cyrus took Babylon he was greeted by the inhabitants as a saviour.

Mesopotamia under Foreign Rulers: Persians and Greeks

With Cyrus's entry into Babylon in 539 BC Mesopotamia became a province of the Persian empire and lost its independence, if not its status as an old and important civilization. Under the Achaemenids Babylonia prospered from farming and trade, and the capital Babylon remained a residence of the kings and an administrative and cultic centre.

A new era began when Alexander the Great took Babylon in 331 BC. From now on Babylonia was a part of the Hellenistic world and Greek influence is visible in various fields. Alexander intended to make Babylon his residence but died before he could realize his plans. His successor, Seleucus I Nicator, founded a new capital on the banks of the Tigris, Seleucia, that under him and the following kings became the political and cultural centre of the Seleucid kingdom and overshadowed Babylon.

During both Achaemenid and Seleucid rulership foreign influences were rather superfluous and the basis of Mesopotamian life was still the old Sumero-Babylonian culture and religion; in general people had good Babylonian names, worshipped Babylonian gods, the social structure still had its roots in the traditional society of Mesopotamia and, even if the everyday language had become Aramaic, the Babylonian literary tradition was still carried on. This changed, however, in the first centuries AD. After the last Seleucid king, Mesopotamia came under the reign of Iranian rulers – the Arsacid or Parthian dynasty – and, although the Greek influence was still strong, both it and the Sumero-Babylonian culture finally vanished during the late Parthian period.

RELIGION

The Sumero-Babylonian Pantheon

Mesopotamian religion was a conglomerate of various religious ideas, gods and myths taken from the different ethnic groups that left their mark on the country. There were sometimes considerable differences in the tradition, not only from one period to the next but also from region to region, due to the origin of the population or the special conditions of life in a certain area, depending on whether the inhabitants were farmers or fishers, nomads or settled.

According to Sumerian mythology history began when An and Uraš, i.e. Heaven and Earth, were separated. Then Heaven fertilized Earth and plants grew up; the first pair of gods, An and Uraš, were thus the parents of vegetation deities and natural forces like Iškur, the thunder or weather god, and of Enlil who was the air and the storm. Enlil and his spouse Ninlil represented the next generation as the parents of the warrior god Ninurta, of the Moon god Nanna, and of gods of the Nether World, among them the god of death, Meslamta'ea (or Nergal). Nanna and his wife Ningal were the parents of the Sun god Utu and the Venus star Inanna, two very important deities in Mesopotamia. In contrast to these awe-inspiring divine powers on whose mercy man was dependent stood Enki, the wise god of magic, always ready to help man. His domain was Abzu, the subterranean fresh waters, and his son was Asalluhi, the divine exorcist.

The Sumerian gods and mythology became amalgamated with the religion of the Akkadians who identified the Sumerian gods with their own deities: Enki with Ea, Nanna with Sin, Utu with Šamaš, and Inanna with Ištar. Cults of former gods disappeared

and new cults prospered, for instance because of political circumstances like the growing importance of Marduk, whose main
sanctuary was Esagila in Babylon, after this city became the
residence of the Babylonian kings. Marduk took over the position
of Enlil as the highest god of the Babylonian pantheon. He is the
hero of the creation epic *Enuma eliš* describing how he fought
the sea monster Tiamat and saved the gods from disaster. As the
son of Enki/Ea Marduk was identified with Asalluhi and therefore
addressed, together with his father, in healing and apotropaic
rituals. In Assyria the god Aššur had a position similar to that of
Marduk in the south. But other gods were worshipped in both
Assyria and Babylonia, like Nabû, son of Marduk and patron god
of scribes, or Enlil's son, the warrior god Ninurta, who, according
to Sumerian myths, defeated the asakku demons and several
monsters. As husband of the healing goddess Gula and as victor
over the evil powers he was invoked to protect mankind against
demons and diseases. Several prayers to the sun god Šamaš as
judge of heaven and earth show his important role in ensuring
that no injustice happened to the poor or the weak, and bringing
deliverance to the afflicted and sick. As goddess of love, Ištar, the
planet Venus, was an important deity, addressed not only in
sexual matters.

Ethics

The gods, as the wise and just rulers of the world who decided
the fate of man, were expected to punish the wicked and protect
the righteous against everything evil: demons, illness, witchcraft
and bad luck in general. This simple idea, that the one who
behaves well will do well, is the basic ethical principle of
Mesopotamian culture, as is also seen in the ideology of kingship.
The just king is like a shepherd to his subjects; he feeds them,
gives them land, protects them against their enemies, acts as a
judge and, not least, serves the gods, from whom he has received
his rulership. If the king fulfils his duties, he and his land are
granted prosperity and wealth as well as peace; if not, the gods
withdraw their support and give the kingship to another who

better deserves it. Thus the ups and downs of history are explained by the morality and integrity of the ruler. A king is victorious because he is righteous and loved by the gods, and is defeated if he commits a serious sin, for instance the neglect of the cult of Marduk in Babylon.

However, the Mesopotamians knew that it was not as simple as that. Ill fortune might very well happen to the just and, conversely, a wicked person might enjoy health and long life. In fact, Sumerian and Akkadian literature tried to explain this apparent contradiction. The rules were so many and complicated that men and women could not know them all and, therefore, it was possible to sin without knowing it and without having any intention to do so. Even the most pious person could not be sure not to transgress a taboo. The ways of the god were past understanding for the people in general; one could at least feel uncertain about what was wrong and what was right. Small things like touching something unclean could be fatal, but how could one know whether an object was clean or unclean? Consciousness of a specific sin could thus be absent, as in the following quotation from a prayer: 'Because of my sin that I know or do not know, I stand before you, o God!' (Ebeling, 1953: 8, lines 10–12). The consequence was that the search for absolution and atonement before the gods could be an almost automatic undertaking; the person in conflict with the gods would try to guard against any transgression, enumerating all possibilities in long lists during the ritual. Otherwise, before doing anything important one sought to get the approval of the gods by the use of divinatory techniques. Of course, seemingly contradictory and unaccountable events could also lead to the pessimistic view that it is of no importance whether one is good or bad, because one may suffer in any case; since the rules of the world are too complicated to discover, there is no point in trying to keep to them (for these themes see Lambert, 1960: 1–20).

According to this view an illness or misfortune was always the result of a disharmony in the relationship man : god, caused by some offence on the side of the human being. Besides medical treatment it was, therefore, absolutely necessary not only to exorcize the evil but also to cleanse the person and reconcile the gods in order to restore the divine protection.

Purification

The main and perhaps the most important action of such a ritual is the purification of the afflicted person. It can for instance be made by sprinkling water, bathing in the river or washing the hands. A basic idea in Mesopotamian religion is the purifying and healing power of water. That this concept is a very old one is shown by some of the earliest Sumerian incantations (*c.* 2600 BC) which invoke the holy and pure water used in magic rituals. The oldest known ritual instruction in Sumerian language concerns a bathing ritual for the king. Note that the god of magic, Enki/Ea, is also the god of fresh water and lives in Abzu, the subterranean ocean. Other methods are wiping the body of the sick person with bread or dough, or rubbing it with oil. As a prophylactic measure purifications were probably carried out regularly in order to avoid attacks of evil demons and diseases.

Magic

Cleansing and prayers were the basic elements in the rituals against witchcraft and all kinds of evil, but, from what we know of them in the first millennium BC, they were combined with numerous and very different actions depending on the situation and purpose; for instance, burning or burying figurines, tying knots, drawing on the ground or on the wall, burning incense or presenting a substitute. They were carried out for an individual in a crisis, i.e. in a state of illness of the body or the mind, or when evil was portended for the person through some sign observed by himself or in his environment. Healing and exorcistic rituals were as a rule performed in the house, on the roof or at the bed of the sick person, and apotropaic rituals often on the bank of the river that was supposed to remove the evil. The methods and purposes of the rituals are very similar, at least in principle, to those known from magic practices in other cultures, both in Antiquity and in European folk belief. The relevant texts are therefore traditionally categorized by Assyriologists as magical literature (see typically Edzard, 1987: 46–7 and Röllig, 1987: 61–4), whereas hymns, myths, prayers, lamentations and records concerning the temple cult are considered, instead, as religion. An important difference, however, is that magical practices in Mesopotamia were not in opposition to an 'official' religion. They were not regarded as superstitious or forbidden, or laughed at. The rituals called 'magical' were the ordinary way of dealing with illness and misfortune and whatever disturbed the relations between man and god. In the eyes of the Mesopotamians they represented an old and divine knowledge and their performers were learned men with a high social status. 'Magic' and 'magical texts' are thus terms used in Assyriological literature for all those texts, namely incantations, apotropaic, exorcistic and purification rituals, and hemerologies★ (as well as some, to our view rather medical, texts that belonged to *āšipūtu*, the exorcist's craft). The large collections of medical recipes, on the other hand, were *asûtu*, the physician's craft. Texts concerning divination by animals' entrails were the competence of the diviner, *bārû*, and astrology and astronomical observations were the responsibility of other experts. This is in accordance with the ancient classification of the texts. The named scholars were highly respected royal servants who advised and informed the king about the perils from evil portents and the movements of the stars. Letters from the exorcists to the king tell us that it was the exorcist's primary task to avert the dangers from the king and the royal family and to carry out the appropriate rituals (see Parpola, 1970). Exorcists participated also in rituals in the temple whenever recitations of incantations and the dispelling of evil were demanded, but there are no records of exorcists treating persons outside the royal court, and we have no information about the performance of the exorcist's rituals in the lower levels of society.

★ See p. 57 below.

THE LITERARY TRADITION

Sumerian Literature

The oldest Sumerian literary texts date from the middle of the third millennium BC. Among them are myths, hymns, epics, proverbs, wisdom texts and incantations, but reading them is difficult, especially because writing in that period was still merely ideographic. Even so, it is possible to state that some of the literary motifs are the same as in more recent texts, and we are therefore justified in talking about a Sumerian literary tradition that begins at least as early as 2600 BC and is continued through the third and second millennium and partly even beyond that.

At the beginning of the second millennium Sumerian was a dead language but as a literary language it was still in use. The Babylonians carefully continued the Sumerian literary tradition and there seems to have been an almost unbroken tradition of 'schools' of scribes (Sumerian: *edubba*) where the students copied the Sumerian texts, learned them by heart, and also composed new literary works. With the end of the Old Babylonian period interest in most of the Sumerian literary compositions decreased and only a small part survived, for instance the myths about the warrior god Ninurta fighting mythical monsters and the *asakku*-demons, together with lamentations and prayers, and large collections of incantations against evil demons, mostly in bilingual versions. The two last-mentioned genres are even known in copies from the Seleucid period. Various compositions were translated into Akkadian, but, even so, the Akkadian versions did not exist as independent texts. A Sumerian text would include an interlinear Akkadian translation which served as an aid for understanding the Sumerian wording as it gradually became foreign and less comprehensible.

Akkadian Literature

The oldest pieces of literature in the Akkadian language are royal inscriptions from the Dynasty of Akkade, but not until the Old

Babylonian period do real literary compositions in this language occur. These include fragments of the Epic of Gilgameš and of the Atra-hasis Epic containing the story of the flood and the creation of man, the Legend of Etana and his flight to heaven, and hymns and incantations. The Akkadian literary works of the Old Babylonian period are original and of a high quality and, although they are naturally influenced by the common Sumero-Akkadian culture, they are never simply translations of Sumerian texts; on the contrary, the narrative has always, in some way or other, been changed. Scholarly works from the Old Babylonian period are, on the other hand, rather few, the most outstanding being collections of omens from extispicy (inspection of entrails for divination). Mathematical texts exist too in considerable number whereas medical, ritual and astrological texts are comparatively rare.

After the decline of the Hammurapi dynasty there was a break in the tradition of literary works. There are only a few sources from Mesopotamia itself, whereas literary texts in Babylonian and Sumerian have been found in Bogazköy, Ras Shamra (Ugarit) and other cities of the Near East dating from the fifteenth and fourteenth centuries BC.

Canonization
During the middle of the second millennium the literary tradition began to be changed. Most parts of the Sumerian compositions were given up, and instead certain genres were preferred and compiled and edited into large series. This process of canonization took place in Babylon under the Kassite kings, probably in the thirteenth century BC. Both Sumerian and Akkadian literary works were standardized; i.e., they were divided into a fixed number of tablets and the succession of incantations or medical recipes in the large collections was established. However, a canonization in the biblical sense was not obtained; the exact wording was still open to changes (see Rochberg–Halton, 1984). A special dialect, so-called Standard Babylonian, was created for these texts and was used even by the Assyrians.

In spite of all the upheavals on the ethnic and political levels the literary tradition thus remained remarkably steady through nearly two thousand years. This outstanding witness to a seemingly exceptional respect for the written word applies to literature in general as well as to religious and scientific texts. Of course some parts of the canon were forgotten, others were added, and both minor and major changes in the texts also occurred, but a large part of the Sumerian and Babylonian texts was still copied, although after the middle of the first millennium BC Aramaic became the spoken vernacular in Assyria and Babylonia. Interestingly, the literary language, whether it was Sumerian, the 'hymnic-epic dialect' of the Old Babylonian period or Standard Babylonian of the first millennium, always differed considerably from the spoken language. Therefore, the written literature as well as scientific texts were understood only by a small group of scholars and scribes, trained in the writing and reading of these special texts.

Babylonian Tradition in Assyria

In Assyria the cultural influence from Babylonia was important and actively supported by some kings who took tablets as booty from Babylon on various occasions. Assurbanipal explicitly ordered that certain literary and scholarly works should be gathered from Babylonian libraries and brought to Nineveh. In Assyria, therefore, large collections with tablets of various genres were created. The most important for the study of magic and witchcraft are a private collection in Aššur belonging to a family of exorcists (seventh century BC) and the library of Assurbanipal in Nineveh; a considerable number of sources comes, in fact, from these two sites. An important collection of literary and magical texts from a temple school in Sultantepe near Harran also dates from the same period. However, not all literary and scholarly texts found in Assyria stem from Babylonia or were copied by Assyrian scribes from Babylonian originals. The Assyrians also created a tradition of their own.

First Millennium

In the second half of the first millennium BC other writing materials became more common for recording Aramaic and Greek texts. Parchments, papyri as well as wax tablets which might have been in use at this time have all perished, either due to destruction in Antiquity or to the humid climate of Mesopotamia. Cuneiform was still written on clay tablets under the Persian and Greek rulers and these later texts are an important source for Mesopotamian cultural and religious life in the Hellenistic period. They are mostly from traditional genres; Babylonian and Sumerian literature, lexical lists, mathematical, astronomical and medical texts, omens, incantations and rituals. The astronomical tradition was continued for the longest time, namely until the first century AD.

To what extent Sumerian or Akkadian texts were translated into Aramaic is hard to say because this language was usually written with an alphabetic script and on the much more perishable parchment, of which practically nothing from this period has survived. Aramaic texts written in cuneiform exist but they are few and show no overwhelming dependence on the Babylonian tradition. To a large extent the old Sumero-Babylonian literary tradition therefore died out when the cuneiform writing was given up.

THE MAGICAL TEXTS

Both Sumerian and Akkadian incantations are attested already in the third millennium, and there are scattered instances of instructions for ritual performances from about the beginning of the second millennium. These texts represent a tradition which was continued in part until Babylonian literature was given up in the last centuries BC (for the early incantations see Farber, 1981; Michalowski, 1985; for the categories of Sumerian incantations see Falkenstein, 1931).

The incantations are, for instance, prophylactic to protect and keep away evil from a person or from the exorcist, or for healing purposes in order to dispel a demon from the body of the patient. The last mentioned include a dialogue between the divine exorcist Asalluhi and his father Enki, god of magic, who gives instructions for magical-medical means to cure the patient. Further, there are incantations for consecrating objects used in a ritual, for instance water and tamarisk for purifications, as well as love charms, incantations against snakes and scorpions, and birth incantations. Sometimes two or three incantations with the same motif were written together on a tablet, and in the Old Babylonian period brief information about the use of the incantation was occasionally added. Later in this millennium the Sumerian incantations were compiled into large series according to their content, and they were provided with Akkadian interlinear translations, for instance the series called The Evil *utukku*-Demons, The *asakku*-Demons and The Headache Demons (for these incantations see Geller, 1985; Thompson, 1903 and 1904). Otherwise, the series of mostly Akkadian incantations like Maqlû ('Burning') and Šurpu (also 'Burning') each render a sequence of prayers and conjurations to be used in one intricate ritual, Maqlû against witchcraft, Šurpu in the case of a person who does not know his offence towards the gods. These series include several tablets each, one of which is the so-called ritual tablet with rather brief instructions for the ritual actions, addressing the exorcist in the second person, e.g., 'you set up an altar'; 'you make a figurine', etc. Other important collections of incantations with ritual instructions are, for instance, *Bit rimki* ('Bath-house'), a bathing and cleansing ceremony for the king performed over several days, perhaps to avert the evil from a moon eclipse, and *Bit mesiri* (lit. 'House of enclosure'), a very complex ritual using numerous figurines and drawings in order to protect a house against every kind of evil (the title alludes to keeping out the evil). It is documented that this ritual too was performed for the king.

By far the greatest number of the magical texts known today date from the Neo-Assyrian period and were found in the libraries of Aššur and Nineveh. The account of Mesopotamian witchcraft and magic given in what follows is primarily based on this material. Although these texts were found in Assyria, some of them stem from Babylonia and the magic tradition was undoubtedly of Babylonian origin.

It is important to note that most of the texts, at least from later periods, were part of royal libraries or belonged to temples or learned scholars, among them exorcists. We are therefore not justified in regarding these texts as part of a popular tradition, although many practices may resemble European folk belief. The fact alone that these texts must have been difficult to understand even for the ancient scholars, written as they were in old and foreign languages, makes it unlikely that they could have been known outside a small number of highly educated experts who apparently served the elite of the society. Some of the texts used by exorcists are explicitly marked as secret knowledge which should not be read by the incompetent; secret texts are primarily collections of commentaries on omens and explanations of incantations and rituals. Apart from the letters containing information about the performance of rituals and the observation of omens and how to react to them, written by exorcists and other scholars to the Assyrian kings Esarhaddon and Assurbanipal (seventh century BC), there are only a few sources for the background of the rituals. Less complicated rituals might well have been performed for members of other social classes, but many questions of this sort remain unanswered.

The performer of magical rituals for healing and apotropaic purposes and for purifications was called *āšipu* or, with a loan word from Sumerian, *mašmaššu*. In what follows both titles are rendered by 'exorcist', an admittedly somewhat incorrect translation because exorcizing demons was not his only task. The *āšipu* was a scholar; his knowledge came for the most part from written sources, although the oral tradition, passed from master to apprentice, was certainly also important. The *āšipu* relied on the text, the fixed wording representing the tradition of the old masters. In the library of the exorcist family in Aššur a catalogue was found with a list of various handbooks of the exorcist's craft 'for teaching and reading' and a similar list ascribed to an ancient scholar Esagil-kîn-apli who probably lived in Babylon in the eleventh century BC (for an edition of this text, *KAR* No. 44,* see Zimmern, 1915–16: 204–13). This text is important as it shows the close connection between the exorcist's craft and Babylon, the city of Marduk, who was also called Asalluhi, the divine exorcist and son of Enki/Ea, the god of magic. Further, the works mentioned in the lists are almost all known to us from copies found in Aššur, Nineveh and other sites and they show us what occupied the exorcist. Most of the quoted series provide means for averting evil of every possible kind; demons, diseases, ghosts and sorcery, as well as the evil portended by certain omens. There are special series for the protection of pregnant women and babies. Moreover, there are prayers to gods, rituals for the purification of buildings, for digging a canal, for the army and for obtaining omens from stars, birds, oxen and cattle. Medical and therapeutic handbooks are also included in the list, as well as compendia of omens of various kind and lists of stones and plants. Most important was probably the diagnostic handbook with the title 'When the exorcist enters the house of a sick person', explaining the reasons for various symptoms and giving prognoses for the recovery of the patient. The author of this work was, according to the tradition, the god Ea, and the already mentioned Esagil-kîn-apli was regarded as its editor (for an edition of the diagnostic handbook see Labat, 1951; for the person of Esagil-kîn-apli see Finkel, 1988). The various handbooks reflect the cosmology of the Mesopotamians, their belief in everything's causality and their striving towards understanding the significance of all events and signs in nature. Lists of good and bad days, observations of natural phenomena, the behaviour of animals, the physiognomy of human beings and the moving of celestial bodies – all these collections contained the basic information to which the exorcist must react. He had to find out whether ill fortune

* For list of Abbreviations, see below p. 94.

was approaching, whether a certain situation or moment was dangerous or not and when and how counteraction was necessary. The exorcist treated sick people and was trained in observing and interpreting physical and psychic symptoms, but in contrast to the practical therapy of the physician who used potions, salves, bandages, etc., the exorcist operated on a metaphysical level by restoring the disturbed relations between human beings and the divine (for exorcist and physician see Ritter, 1965).

Mesopotamian Magic, State of Research

Numerous tablets containing incantations against witchcraft and evil demons, excavated in Nineveh in the nineteenth century, were quoted, in part, as early as 1874 by François Lenormant in *La magie chez les chaldéens et les origines accadiennes*. Scholarly editions of these important texts were already published at the turn of the twentieth century, for instance, *Maqlû* by Tallqvist in 1895, and the collections of bilingual incantations against demons by Thompson in 1903–4. Since then a large number of similar texts has been excavated in other Mesopotamian sites as well as in neighbouring countries, and new and revised editions of these sources have continuously been made. However, editing a cuneiform text is complicated and time-consuming, since the text has to be reconstructed from numerous fragments, often dispersed in museums all over the world. Therefore, many texts have still not been translated or published with a copy of the cuneiform tablet, and no modern edition of even important rituals like *Bit mesiri* exists.

In spite of the many highly competent publications of the Mesopotamian magical texts, theoretical studies have been neglected and there is no modern, comprehensive study of this material. In the Assyriological literature about incantations and their rituals authors usually confine themselves to commentaries on grammatical and lexical problems, and little room is left for discussion of the content and background. There has been little or no consideration of the techniques of Mesopotamian magic or theorizing about its nature and history, and studies of themes such as its relationship to magic in other cultures, both contemporary and later (e.g. Hittite, Persian, European) are still to be done.

WITCHCRAFT

References to actually executed witchcraft are very few, instructions for performing evil magic do not exist and only one case of a recorded court trial concerning witchcraft has so far been found. This is in striking contrast to the comprehensive material concerning incantations, rituals and medical recipes against witchcraft which document a profound fear of being bewitched. There is no doubt that witchcraft in ancient Mesopotamia was forbidden and strongly punished if detected as described in the law codes, but the law texts also show that measures against unjustified accusations were necessary since a suspicion of witchcraft was easily raised but very difficult to prove. In the anti-witchcraft texts there are many detailed descriptions of the methods and effects of witchcraft but no instructions for discovering a witch, for instance by magical means or by divination. In most cases the witch obviously remained anonymous, nor does it seem to have been necessary for the success of a ritual against witchcraft to name the witch. At all events, the gods invoked to dissolve the witchcraft were believed to know the identity of the evildoer and with the divine destruction of his (or her) evil intentions a trial in court and a confrontation with the adversary was possibly made less urgent. Certainly, a person who was thought to be bewitched would often have a concrete suspicion as to who his enemy was, but for social reasons it was probably wiser not to utter it.

A Literary Example of Witchcraft

The Sumerian epic called 'Enmerkar and Ensuhkešdanna' describes a magic competition between an evil sorcerer (Sumerian: *maš-maš*) and an old woman who at last defeats the wizard. The situation is described in various epic tales: Ensuhkešdanna,

the ruler of the legendary city Aratta, located somewhere to the
east of Sumer, wanted Uruk to submit, but Enmerkar, the
sovereign of this city, went with his troops to conquer Aratta and
in all versions he ends up as the victor. In this epic the struggle is
conducted with magical weapons. First, Ensuhkešdanna sends his
ambassador to Uruk demanding a tribute and when Enmerkar
refuses Ensuhkešdanna gets angry and, on the advice of his
minister, delegates a magician who will force Uruk to submit by
magical means. The magician goes to Sumer, but unexpectedly
he does not stop in Uruk but in a neighbouring town, Ereš, the
city of the grain goddess Nisaba. Here he goes to the stable and
sheepfold and with a magic formula he prevents the cow and
goat from producing milk:

> (The *maš-maš*) approached the cattle-pen, the house where
>   the cows live,
> The cow in the cattle-pen shook its head at him,
> He talked to the cow, he conversed with it as if it were a
>   human being:
> 'Cow, who eats your fat? Who drinks your milk?'

The cow answers that both the fat and milk as well as other dairy
products are for the goddess Nisaba, whereupon the *maš-maš*
utters a curse: 'Cow, your fat to your shining horns, your milk to
your back!' In the sheepfold the magician does the same with the
goat and from this moment the cow and goat cannot produce
milk. When the calves and kids are almost starving the cowherd
and the shepherd pray to the sun god. This passage is fragmentary
but somehow, apparently in answer to their prayer, a wise
woman, Sagburru, is introduced who enters into a magical
competition with the *maš-maš*. They both throw a bait into the
river and first the magician pulls out a carp, then Sagburru pulls
out an eagle that seizes the carp. Next time the magician pulls
out a ewe and its lamb, and the wise woman a wolf that seizes
both ewe and lamb. The competition goes on in this way three
times more, the animals getting bigger and more dangerous, until
the magician declares he is beaten and the woman exclaims:

'Sorcerer, you may have magical power, but where is your sense?'
Although the *maš-maš* begs for his life Sagburru kills him and
throws his body into the river. When Ensuhkešdanna learns about
this he acknowledges the superiority of Enmerkar and Uruk and
the epic ends by declaring Enmerkar as the winner and by praising
Nisaba (edition of this epic in Berlin, 1979; for the sections dealt
with here, see pp. 50–7).

Two things must be noted here; first, the magician, here
performing witchcraft, is called *maš-maš* which later on becomes
the title of an official occupied with healing and purification
rituals; secondly, the sorcerer is defeated by a woman, who,
although she uses magic as well, is not called witch or *maš-maš*
but um.ma which denotes a wise woman, often but not necessarily an old woman. The term is sometimes applied to goddesses,
for instance Inanna.

Laws against Witchcraft
The Laws are not directly occupied with the penalty for witchcraft but rather with the problems of proving a charge concerning
witchcraft. Such cases are dealt with in two codes of the laws of
ancient Mesopotamia: Codex Hammurapi, eighteenth century
BC, and the Middle Assyrian Laws, probably from the twelfth
century BC.

Codex Hammurapi §2:

> If a man has brought a charge of sorcery against another man,
> but has not proved it (by means of witnesses), the one against
> whom the charge of sorcery was brought will go to the river
> of the ordeal (and) undergo the river ordeal and, if the river
> overcomes him, his accuser shall take over his house. If the
> river ordeal clears that man and he comes out safely, the one
> who brought the charge of sorcery shall be put to death; he
> who leapt into the holy river shall take over the house of his
> accuser.
> (cf. Driver and Miles, 1952 and 1955 for edition and commen-
> tary of Codex Hammurapi)

The Middle Assyrian Laws §47:

If either a man or a woman have made magical preparations and they have been seized in their hands (and) charge (and) proof have been brought against them, the maker of the magical preparations shall be put to death.

The man who saw the making of the magical preparations (and) heard from the mouth of an eye-witness of the magical preparations who told him, (saying) 'I myself saw (it)', shall come forward (as) an earwitness (and) tell the king; if what he has told the king is denied by the eyewitness, he shall make a statement in the presence of the Bull, the son of the sun-god, saying: 'On my oath, he said (it)'; (and then) he is quit. (As for) the eyewitness who told (it) and denied (it) – the king shall interrogate him as he thinks fit (and) shall read his inmost thoughts. The exorcist, when he is fetched, shall make the man speak, and the former shall speak, saying: 'From the adjuration, wherewith thou hast been adjured before (?) the king and his son, they will not release thee; thou hast surely been adjured according to the words of the tablet wherewith thou hast been adjured before(?) the king and his son.
(Driver and Miles, 1935: 414–17; for legal commentary see pp. 118–26)

Whereas the later law code orders a thorough examination and interrogation of the involved persons, the earlier one pre-scribes a river-ordeal for the case if no evidence or witness can prove the question of guilt. River-ordeal was a method to decide a lawsuit when no evidence or witnesses were available. (For the use of ordeal in ancient Mesopotamia see Frymer-Kensky, 1977; Driver and Miles, 1935: 83–106.) The law codes provide river-ordeal only in a few cases. Besides witchcraft, a woman who was accused of adultery, for instance, should go to the river to prove her innocence. But it is also attested that the parties in a court trial would undergo the river-ordeal for the sake of the ownership of a slave, a field or a sheep. In such cases one or both parties were requested either to swear on their statements before the god in the temple, or undergo the river-ordeal. Oath and river-ordeal were not compulsory, at least not in all cases, since it is attested that persons refused to swear or to go to the river. The one who refused was the loser and had to renounce his claim.

How the ordeal was actually carried out is not clear, since both law texts and juridical documents are short and not precise in their formulation. The question is whether the guilty or the innocent party sank or floated in the water. This is a matter of interpretation of the Akkadian verbs which are here translated as 'overcome' (guilty) and 'come out safely' (innocent). It is often assumed that when the river 'overcomes' the guilty, it means that he drowns and thus is executed on the spot, whereas 'come out safely' means that the innocent comes out of the water, i.e. floating on the water. (For this discussion see Driver and Miles, 1935: 94–6; and, more recently, von Weiher, 1981.) This is a possible reading of the wording of Codex Hammurapi §2 but perhaps less likely, since river-ordeal in other cultures of the Near East operated differently. Here, the accused person was regarded as innocent if he sank into the water, since it meant that the river accepted him; on the contrary, if he floated on the water he was thought to be rejected by the river god and thus guilty. Moreover, the ordeal was not a punishment but a method for deciding the question of guilt. Therefore, although this is nowhere explicitly said, the persons were most likely recovered from the water in *both* cases, whereupon the guilty one would be punished according to the law. In the case of sorcery the penalty was certainly death, as in the Assyrian Laws, since the accuser was put to death if his accusation was not supported by the river-ordeal.

As mentioned at the beginning, court trials against witches are not attested, but a possible exception is a case from the Old Babylonian period in which a man accuses his daughter-in-law and her mother of sorcery in a dispute concerning barley. (The documents concerning this case are published in Walters, 1970.) The accuser's son had planted a field with grain but, as the field was lent to a tenant farmer, the father did not receive his share of the crop. In a confrontation between father and son before the judges of the city the father said: 'I will put a stop to your wife and your mother-in-law, your sorceresses.' The son promptly answered: 'And I will put a stop to your sorceress.' The case went to the mayor and elders of the city who together with the judges were supposed to settle it. Unfortunately, the end of this trial as well as the sentence are unknown. It seems that the father was upset because the son acted against his instructions and he blamed the son's wife and mother-in-law for this rebellion against fatherly authority. It is not clear whether it was thought that some magic rites had brought this about; probably, the trial was initiated because of the question of the ownership of the barley and was not a real witchcraft trial at all.

THE WITCH

Although anti-witchcraft texts are almost never concerned with the question of the witch's identity, it was probably not unusual to suspect an individual person. For instance, it is occasionally stated that the name of the witch was to be written on the figurine used in the ritual, and this may have been the normal practice even if it is not always written explicitly in the instructions. Also, in a recipe, the drugs to be worn in a leather bag around the neck are said to be directed against the evil machinations of a man's wife (a wife using witchcraft is mentioned as well in other contexts). More striking, however, is the frequent expression in Maqlû and other similar incantations: 'Who are you, sorceress?', or, addressing a god: 'You know them (the witches) I do not know them!' The reason for the anonymity of the witches in these cases could possibly be that Maqlû was performed, not in a situation where witchcraft was actually suspected, but regularly at a certain time of the year, perhaps at the end of the month of Ab when the moon disappears, a time which was thought especially dangerous for the king and demanded exceptional protection (this was suggested by Abusch, 1974). Maqlû was thus directed against every thinkable witch, known and unknown, male and female, with various professions, names and nationalities being mentioned as well.

In an incantation the sorceress may be identified as a foreigner from Elam, Gutium, Sutium, Lullubu or Hanigalbat. One also finds the phrase: 'They practise witchcraft, constantly they practise witchcraft, the Gutian (women), the Elamite (women), the daughters of the women of Hanigalbat' (Maqlû IV 119–23 and 105–6, see Meier, 1937: 32–3). These were lands traditionally in conflict with the rulers of Mesopotamia, but in the Neo-Assyrian period, at the time when these texts were written, they were, with the exception of Elam, no longer real enemy countries. The mentioning of these peoples could be due to a bias against foreigners in general, but it may also reflect the fact that a part of the magic tradition in Mesopotamia had its origin in Elam (cf. Haas, 1980; van Dijk, 1987).

Almost nothing is known about which members of Mesopo-tamian society were able, or thought to be able, to perform witchcraft. Some practices may have been common knowledge, while others, like rituals with figurines and incantations, perhaps in foreign languages, were certainly matters for an expert. Incan-tations sometimes identify the witch as belonging to professions which are rarely attested or little known, like snake charmer and ecstatic; on one occasion, the sorceress is called exorcist (Maqlû III 40–5 and IV 124–8, see Meier, 1937: 23, 33). However, as long as there are no surviving reports of real cases of witchcraft it is highly uncertain whether these descriptions are realistic or purely literary. A commission to carry out witchcraft is mentioned in Maqlû: 'The one who has performed evil magic against me (. . .), who said to the witch: "Bewitch!", who said to the sorceress: "Make evil magic!"' (Maqlû III 118–22, see Meier, 1937: 25–6).

The Mesopotamian material mentions both male and female witches; for instance, in the anti-witchcraft rituals pairs of figu-rines (i.e. male and female) are often represented to the god:

Supreme Girru, pure god! Now I have made before your great
divinity two figurines of copper (representing) my sorcerer and
my sorceress!
(Maqlû II 89–91, see Meier, 1937: 16)

However, allusions to women using evil magic are in the
majority. This is probably due to the social situation of women
in Mesopotamia. After her marriage, a woman lived with the
family of her husband and being a stranger there she was easily
suspected. Women also had few privileges and little means to
assert their rights, so witchcraft could be a tempting possibility.
Evil magic seems to have been the weapon of the weak, of
women and persons in lower social positions who were not able
to get at their adversaries by legal means. (For women and
witchcraft see Rollin, 1983.)

HOW WITCHCRAFT MANIFESTS ITSELF

The suspicion of being bewitched probably arose when a person
had serious and recurrent conflicts with other people combined
with the occurrence of certain physical symptoms. A concrete
threat uttered by an adversary like 'I shall bewitch you!' is of
course imaginable, if not likely, considering the punishment for
sorcery. In some few cases it is noted in the ritual texts that
witchcraft 'has been seen'. It is not completely clear what this
involves, but perhaps some *materia magica*, like a dead animal, or
other objects were placed before the house of the victim. Such
concrete and unmistakable signs of evil magic being performed
were, it seems, characteristic of the special type of sorcery called
'cutting the throat' (*zikurudû*), which is more fully described
below. In omen compendia there are a few instances of portents
announcing witchcraft. These texts give little information about
the threatening evil but merely state that if this and this sign is
observed the man (for whom the omen is being taken), or his
house, is bewitched. Compendia of later periods can be more

detailed; for example, if a certain feature on the left side of the entrails looks like a fish, 'the wife of the man will bewitch him' (CT 20 plate 43 col. I 4); or, concerning the method used by the witch, if, on a certain part of the sheep's liver, the appearance of a design resembles entwined snakes it means that 'from the house of the man a sorceress will take dust from the footsteps of the man for (performing) witchcraft' (BRM 4 no. 12, lines 74–5). An unusual text describes how to obtain an omen to decide whether impotence is caused by witchcraft or is of some other nature:

> You mix together dough (made of) emmer and potter's clay; you make figurines of the man and the woman, put them one upon the other, and place them at the man's head, then recite [the incantation] seven times; you remove (them) and [put them near] a pig. If the pig approaches, (it means) 'Hand of Ištar'; (if) the pig does not approach [the figurines], (it means) that the man has been affected by sorcery.
> (*KAR* no. 70, 6–10, see Biggs, 1967: 46)

It seems surprising that there are rather few instances of such omens but, obviously, the common method of diagnosing witchcraft was observation of the physical and psychical condition of the patient, and this is described in numerous medical and ritual texts. The effects of evil magic manifested themselves in many ways; they could be light and rather easy to overcome, and they could be fatal. Sometimes a potion would be enough to cure a bewitched person, as several recipes in the medical series 'To dissolve Witchcraft' show; also, certain rituals were claimed to protect a person against witchcraft for the rest of his life. However, the evil magic might be so dangerous that the death of the patient was beyond doubt and the exorcist was recommended not even to try a cure: 'His illness is "Hand of Mankind", a figurine of him was placed (in a grave). The exorcist shall not perform any ritual for his recovery' (Labat, 1951: 176–7, lines 2–3).

Diagnosis

Curing a bewitched patient was a matter for either a physician or an exorcist. The former used medications made of herbs, oils, pulverized stones and many other ingredients for potions, salves or amulets to wear around the neck. The latter, who possibly took charge only when the situation was rather serious, performed rituals with offerings and prayers, burning of figurines representing the assumed witches and purification of the patient. In the medical recipes as well as in the ritual instructions detailed descriptions of the symptoms are recorded, but attempts to systematize the various indications are only sporadic. In one of the exorcist's handbooks, called 'When the exorcist enters the house of a sick person' (Labat, 1951), symptoms in almost every part of the body are described with many variations. Each description ends with a prognosis, e.g. 'he will recover', or 'he will die', or, with some details, 'the illness will be hard, but then he will recover', or 'he will die within 30 days'. In many instances the source of the illness is explained; it is caused by an angry god, a demon or a ghost, due to some wrong that the patient has done. In more than half of the cases a god was thought responsible for the illness; ghosts account for about a fifth, and various demons for most of the rest. Witchcraft, however, is mentioned in less than 5 per cent of the instances, although there are a lot of incantations, rituals and medical texts to avert evil magic. The reasons for this are not evident. Perhaps the scholarly literature, like the just-mentioned handbook of the exorcist as well as the omen compendia, represents a different tradition that was primarily occupied with other themes, like the disturbed relations between the gods and the human world. In practice, however, numerous examples of rituals and medications against witchcraft apparently show that people in general had a real fear of being bewitched, a fear which might affect both their physical and psychical condition and made counter-measures necessary.

Characteristic Symptoms

Some of the symptoms of witchcraft are characteristic and occur again and again; the bewitched person is confused, forgets what he is talking about, is terrified, is not taken seriously by those around him, he has fever, or serious pains, he is hungry but cannot eat, or he is gnawing his teeth while sleeping. It is often psychic disturbances which indicate evil magic, such as a speech defect, forgetfulness or absent-mindedness:

> If a man – when he speaks, his saliva runs, (and) he sprays spittle in the face of another man, if he forgets his words, if his mouth 'disappears', if his mouth . . . (uncertain): this man has been given something malicious (? unclear, lit.: treacherous talk) to eat.
>
> (*BAM* II no. 161, II 16'–21', with duplicate *BAM* V no. 436, VI' 12'–15')

Slobbering was also a frequent symptom, but it was not a particularly dangerous effect of witchcraft since it could be cured by means of a potion, as in the following example from a medical handbook:

> If a man – saliva in his mouth cannot be stopped: This man is bewitched. In order to cure him you pound together (the plants) *elikulla* and *maštakal* (and) [let him drink them] in first-quality beer.
>
> (*AMT* no. 31,4 obv. 14–15, see Thomsen, 1987: 51 and note 120)

There is also a more detailed description in the diagnostic handbook 'When the exorcist enters the house of a sick man':

> If his arms and knees are constantly exhausted, if he at once has ejaculation (and) his saliva runs in his bed, if he at other times is lame and his abdomen has fever: witchcraft holds this man; the same: a ghost holds him.
>
> (Labat, 1951: 88–9, lines 8–10)

Like the flowing saliva, constant or uncontrollable flow of semen is a sign of witchcraft and normally means that the semen of the man in question has been put in a grave. This type of witchcraft causes impotence. Similarly it is a sign of witchcraft when much liquid comes from the vagina: 'If a woman has been given drugs of hate to eat and much water runs of her vagina' (diagnosis in *BAM* III no. 237, IV 29).

Babies might also be victims of witchcraft, showing similar symptoms. The diagnostic handbook ascribes nervousness, anxiety and slow physical development to evil magic:

> If a baby's intestines are bloated and it does not eat when the breast is offered to it: a sorceress is chosen (as spouse) for this baby. If a baby, while it is asleep, turns; or if it finds no relief and constantly frets: the *šulhu*-disease, caused by witchcraft, has affected it. (. . .) If a baby has been nursed three months (but) its hands and feet are still contorted and its muscles are weak: (already) in the womb of its mother the *šulhu*-disease, caused by witchcraft, has affected it.
> (Labat, 1951: 218–19, lines 15–19)

The symptoms referred to and quoted above are all characteristic of witchcraft diagnosis and mostly reappear word-for-word in various anti-witchcraft texts, sometimes in longer descriptions. However, many of them are also found in different contexts as symptoms caused by ghosts or by quite different diseases.

These matter-of-fact descriptions in the technical literature can be compared with the more poetic, and pathetic, wording in prayers and incantations, describing physical pains and conflicts with other people as a result of evil magic and recited in rituals. An example is the prayer addressed to the gods of the night (i.e. the stars) at the beginning of the long and complicated ritual called *Maqlû*:

> I have called the evening, the midnight and the dawn,
> Because a witch has bewitched me,
> A deceitful woman has betrayed me.

They drove my god and my goddess away from me,
To those who see me I have become displeasing,
I am afflicted, I cannot rest, day or night,
They filled my mouth with threads,
They took away flour (for offerings) from my mouth,
They diminished my drinking water,
My joyous song (has become) lamentation, my happiness
     mourning.
(Maqlû I 3–12, see Meier, 1937: 7)

Similarly, there is a prayer to Marduk, pleading for help and
recovery from all possible evils:

The demon *Alû*, headache, suffering, skin disease,
     depression[?],
A virulent disease, curse, (and) oath overwhelmed me;
The (earlier) perfection of my body is afflicted, I am
     covered with disease as with a garment;
They (the witches) have taken figurines representing me
     (and) put them [in a grave],
Dust of my feet has been collected, my measures have been
     taken;
My dignity is carried away, I am afflicted and defiled by
     evil machinations of human beings;
Anger of gods and human beings is upon me, terrifying are
     my dreams, evil (and) wrong are
My portents, my omens are confused and allow no reliable
     decision.
(*BMS* no. 12 lines 51–8, translation in Falkenstein and von
     Soden, 1953: 304)

METHODS

In cuneiform literature no instructions for performing evil magic
have been found so far, but in medical texts, rituals and incantations directed against witchcraft there are many allusions to the

techniques and means by which the sorcerer was thought to make his evil intentions effective. Witchcraft could operate in various ways – through direct contact, for instance with unclean water or bewitched food, or indirectly through actions mostly with images representing the victim. Negative feelings and actions alone were also claimed to have some effect, as in the case of the well-known belief in the evil eye. Most of these methods have parallels in the techniques used by the exorcist in anti-witchcraft as well as in other rituals.

Contagious Magic

The evil magic is transferred to a person by contact with an unclean or somehow poisoned object, for instance water: 'The sorceresses poured their witchcraft in (dirty) water over me' (prayer to the god Nabû, *STT* I no. 65 line 41); '(The witches) washed me with dirty water, they anointed me with a salve made of evil herbs' (Maqlû I 105–6, see Meier, 1937: 11). The effects of evil magic are also transferred by food. How this was thought to occur is unknown, but the belief seems widespread. There is an example in the diagnostic handbook: 'If the patient, while he is talking, once and again interrupts himself(?): this man has been given bewitched food to eat in order to get *maštaqtu* (a physical deficiency)' (Labat, 1951: 176–7, line 5), and another in Maqlû: 'The witches gave me bewitched food to eat, gave me bewitched water to drink' (Maqlû I 103–4, see Meier, 1937: 11). From Sultantepe comes a small tablet with two medications against this type of witchcraft: 'If a man has pains between his shoulders and his teeth are bleeding – this man has a pulmonary disease, he has been given something bewitched to eat or to drink' (*STT* I no. 102, lines 1–6). For his recovery beads of certain stones are strung on a thread of red and white wool and laid around the patient's neck, while some plants are crushed to be drunk in beer or sweet wine in the morning on an empty stomach. The second recipe is very similar. This time the crushed plants are put in beer and placed 'under the stars' until next morning, then the patient should drink it on an empty stomach and vomit. The latter recipe was quite popular; at least it is duplicated in two texts from Aššur (*BAM* II no. 190, lines 22–6 and *BAM* II no. 193 II 2'–7'). Moreover, a tablet from Nineveh has exactly the same symptoms with a diverging recipe; a plant, either *arihu* or *matqu*, is crushed and drunk with vinegar or put into the anus, probably as an enema (*AMT* No. 48, 2, lines 1–5). The effect of the remedy is in all cases the same – to get rid of the bewitched food.

Magic Knots

Incantations, in their poetic rather than concrete language, frequently mention knots and ties by which the witch holds her victim captive; for example, the phrase 'I break your ties!' is used as a refrain (Maqlû VII 93–100, see Meier, 1937: 50), and 'Untie these knots which surround me!' is recited seven times before Sin in order to avert evil magic of the type *zikurudû* (*BAM* V no. 449 col. II 1). Of course, these expressions could be metaphors for the condition of a person fearing witchcraft, but, in fact, tying knots on strings of wool, sometimes with certain colours, is known as well from many rituals and magical therapies; for instance against symptoms in the forehead: 'You spin together red wool, white wool, gazelle sinew and "male" rush, you tie seven and seven knots (. . .), you recite the incantation seven times, you touch it with cedar "blood" (and) bind it around his forehead' (*AMT* no. 103 col. II 14–17); or against a ghost: 'You spin together combed wool and red wool, you tie seven knots (. . .), you recite the incantation (and) bind it around his forehead, then you let him say thus: "Until the red becomes white (and) the white becomes red, the ghost that has appeared to me shall not return"' (Castellino, 1955: 254–5, lines 44–9). Evil knots were probably thought to be made in a similar way; they could be undone by gods, as in the prayer to the moon god Sin quoted above, or destroyed by the Fire god. In the instructions for the ritual Maqlû, binding knots in order to undo witchcraft is mentioned only once. First, three knots are tied on a string of white wool, then seven knots, also on a white wool string; the incantation accompanying the latter action speaks of untying evil

knots. The strings are probably burnt together with the figurines
and plants and symbolize the destroying of the evil magic:

> They practise witchcraft, constantly they practise witchcraft,
> the Gutian (women), the Elamite (women),
> the daughters of the women of Hanigalbat.
> Six in the land make ties,
> Six in number are their ties, seven in number are my
>   loosening.
> What they perform during the night, at day I dissolve it;
> What they perform all day, during the night I dissolve it.
> I place them in the mouth of the Fire god who consumes,
>   burns, binds (and) overcomes the sorceresses.
> (Maqlû IV 105–16, see Meier, 1937: 32)

Evil Magic with Images

Perhaps the most common way to perform witchcraft was
thought to be the use of images made of clay or other materials
like tallow, wax, cedar wood or dough, and mixed or decorated
with objects taken from the victim – hair, saliva, semen, a piece
of clothing and even dust from his footsteps. These objects alone,
without making figurines of them, could also be used for evil
magic. There are many allusions to this in the incantations against
witchcraft. A typical accusation is, for instance: '(The witches)
have placed dust of my feet in a grave, have taken my measurements, have collected dust on which my feet have stepped, have
taken my spittle, have plucked out my hair, have cut off my hem'
(*KAR* no. 80, lines 30–3). Here is a more elaborate example,
taking every possibility into account in the list of the evil deeds
of the witches:

> You (the witches) have picked me out for a dead body,
> You have handed me over to a skull,
> You have handed me over to a ghost of my kin,
> You have handed me over to a ghost of a foreigner,
> To a roving ghost for whom nobody cares,

You have handed me over to the plain, the open country,
the desert,
You have handed me over to the wall and parapet,
You have handed me over to the Lady of the plain and
the open country,
You have handed me over to the oven for roasted barley,
the baking oven, the kiln, the bellows,
You have given figurines of me to a dead man,
You have picked out my figurines for a dead man,
You have placed figurines of me with a dead man,
You have placed figurines of me in the lap of a dead man,
You have buried figurines of me in a grave of a dead man,
You have given figurines of me to a skull,
You have enclosed figurines of me in a wall,
You have placed figurines of me at the threshold,
You have immured figurines of me in the drainage
opening of the [city] wall,
You have buried figurines of me on a causeway so that
people have stepped upon them,
Figurines of me, made of tamarisk or cedar wood, of
tallow, wax, residue of linseed, bitumen, clay or dough,
Figurines of me resembling my face and my body you
have made
And given them to a dog or a pig to eat,
Or to the birds of heaven to eat, or you have thrown them
into the river,
You have give figurines of me to Lamaštu, the daughter of
Heaven,
You have given figurines of me to the Fire god.
(Maqlû IV 17–47, see Meier, 1937: 29–30)

According to these and other incantations against witchcraft, figurines were either destroyed, for instance burnt in an oven, dissolved in water, or trodden upon, or left in a desert place exposed to dangerous demons, buried in a grave so that a ghost might take hold of the victim, or placed in a drainage opening to be polluted by its water. To give a person to the demon Lamaštu, who afflicts children, or to Ereškigal, the queen of the land of the dead, or to the Fire god was, in each case, simply a metaphor for similar actions. The possibilities were numerous, all indicating that what happened to a figurine was transferred to the person it represented. The intention behind these actions was to make the victim unclean and unpleasant to the gods and deprive him of divine protection, resulting in failing health and mental disturbances. This effect was certainly not to be achieved solely by actions with the figurines. No doubt the witch was also assumed to invoke a god, bring offerings and recite incantations. At least, the bewitched person asks for the undoing of both words and actions: 'May their word be dispelled but my word not! The word that I speak: may their word not block my word!' (Maqlû I 70–1, see Meier, 1937: 9). One incantation is described as for 'immediately binding the mouth (of a sorceress)' (Lambert, 1957–8: 296: B rev. 28).

The success of a ritual depended on the god's compliance and his readiness to help by purifying, exorcizing or healing the person in question. In the same way, presumably, the witch had to call on divine powers for assistance, but, as far as we know, there was no special god for black magic; rather, any deity could probably be addressed. At least, requests expressed in prayers that a god should not listen to the witches indicate this:

> Put muzzles on the mouths of my sorcerer and my sorceress!
> Throw the incantation of the wise one among the gods,
>   Marduk!
> If they call you, do not answer them,
> If they talk to you, do not listen to them!
> (Maqlû I 54–47, see Meier, 1937: 9)

Direct information about which gods were addressed by the witches is sparse. However, in one diagnosis Ištar and Dumuzi are unmistakably identified as the gods whom the witch has invoked and the anti-witchcraft ritual is also performed before these gods: 'Against this man witchcraft has been made before

Ištar and Dumuzi and figurines representing him have been placed in a grave' (Farber, 1977: 227, lines 9–10). As one of the symptoms is impotence it is clear that Ištar was addressed because of her influence over sexual matters, and it is also well known that prayers to Ištar are recited *against* impotence. That witchcraft could, or had to, be dispelled by the god before whom it was performed is also supported by other cases; for instance, rituals against sorcery of the type *zikurudû* made before a certain star are carried out before that same star.

Messages of Witchcraft: zikurudû

A special type of witchcraft was called *zikurudû* from Sumerian zi kud-ru-da, 'cutting the throat' (see Thomsen, 1987: 40–7). Characteristically it was 'seen', apparently as a sign or object of some sort placed where the victim could not miss seeing it. The bewitched person would thus know that evil magic had been carried out even before he suffered from its consequences, in contrast to the other cases where specific physical symptoms indicated that witchcraft had been performed. What such a sign was is not completely clear; sometimes a small animal is mentioned and it has been proposed that an animal's skin was filled with some magical materials and placed in or before the victim's house (Köcher, 1980: p. XVI note 26). This is very possible but no descriptions exist of such a method, and what was involved might just as well, therefore, have been simply an observation of an animal behaving in an extraordinary way but understood as an evil portent. *Zikurudû* was mostly performed in the night before certain stars, and rituals against it were likewise carried out in front of the same stars, for instance the Great Bear, Scorpio or Sirius. Šamaš and Sin were also addressed in order to dispel *zikurudû*, for instance in the following instructions on a tablet from Nineveh:

> If *zikurudû* has been made against a man and it has been visible: You take this evil magic which was seen (and) place it before Šamaš, you tell Šamaš your worries.

Before Šamaš you slaughter a pig upon this evil magic; this evil magic you put into a pig's skin. Before Šamaš you let the man against whom *zikurudû* was made say as follows:

'Šamaš, the *zikurudû* magic which was made – he has not seen it, (but) I have seen it!'

You let him say this seven times before Šamaš; every day [he should tell Šamaš] his worries. This evil magic which is in the pig's skin [. . . rest is broken].
(*BAM* V No. 449 col. I 1–9)

A similar kind of evil magic is probably meant by the expression 'leather bag of witchcraft', this being perhaps a bag or simply a piece of leather tied around drugs or other objects. There is one reference to instructions against the appearance of such bags: 'If a man, either on the field, in the open country or in the plain, sees a bag with evil magic' (*KAR* No. 72 rev. 18–19, see Ebeling, 1954: 186–7; the tablet with the counteractions is not preserved).

The Evil Eye

Sometimes neither direct contact nor complicated rituals were required in order to harm a person; merely an evil eye, pointing with an 'evil finger', evil words or feelings had the power to injure. These phenomena are often met with in enumerations of various evils: 'Evil man, evil eye, evil mouth, evil tongue, evil spell, witchcraft, spittle, evil machinations, go out of the house!' or: 'May the evil eye, the evil mouth, the evil tongue, the evil lips stand aside!' (see Thomsen, 1992: 21–2).

Belief in the evil eye is perhaps the most common of these, known in nearly every corner of the world. In Mesopotamia, however, there are surprisingly few incantations or medical prescriptions against it, compared with the numerous materials against witchcraft in general. This is most probably due to the less dangerous character of the effects of the evil eye. As the Sumerian incantations show, the evil eye brought rather harmless, everyday accidents; a tool or a pot was broken, clothes were torn, food was spoiled and the like. This might be serious and annoying enough but as a rule it did not require complicated and expensive rituals or the assistance of an exorcist and this is most likely the reason why only a few texts against the evil eye are found among the handbooks of the magical experts. Protection was, for instance, given by amulets, i.e. certain stones, probably in eye shape.

ANTI-WITCHCRAFT RITUALS

Medical Treatment of Witchcraft

In order to cure the consequences of witchcraft a physician knew medicines and therapies of different kinds. Among the medical handbooks from Neo-Assyrian Aššur and Nineveh there are large tablets with varied recipes against witchcraft. Sometimes they give detailed descriptions of the symptoms and type of witchcraft, or it is simply stated 'if a man is bewitched' and then the recipe is provided. In yet other cases lists of plants, stones and other substances end with the declaration: 'Plants (or stones) to dissolve witchcraft". In some collections recipes against witchcraft appear alongside others against diseases due to ghosts or demons. In other instances a whole tablet is devoted to the treatment of impotence, often assumed to be caused by evil magic. There are also handbooks which are organized according to the parts of the body, dealing for instance with diseases of the head, eyes, heart and feet etc., where witchcraft may be only one among several other diagnoses for certain symptoms. The great variety of the medical therapies demonstrates that many different sources and traditions have been combined in these handbooks, but it also shows that there was no particular plant or stone, potion or salve which alone could counteract evil magic. The choice of medication and therapy was dependent on the character of the symptoms and the type of witchcraft diagnosed.

The recipes vary from rather simple ones with a couple of ingredients only, to those containing up to fifty herbs, minerals and other substances. Typically they were to be drunk with beer

or wine, but they could also be prepared with oil for a salve. The
herbs are, as a rule, those to which a purifying quality in general
was ascribed, like tamarisk or seeds of tamarisk, juniper and a
plant called 'it heals a thousand (diseases)'. In one case the potion
is to be drunk from a spoon of tamarisk wood. Since most of the
Babylonian plant names are not identified, little can be said about
the real content of these medications. However, the most frequently mentioned herbs and spices are probably mint, turmeric
and thyme. Animal parts also occur in the prescriptions; for
instance, the kidney of a young lamb which had not yet eaten
grass was dried and crushed and used for a bath, or garlic was
eaten with beer mash. Even a bone from a dead man was used in
one medication, and necklaces with certain stones could protect
against witchcraft. In some cases the recitation of, mostly rather
short, incantations is prescribed. (There is no edition of the
medical handbooks concerning witchcraft but parts of them are
translated in Thompson, 1930, especially pp. 11–15.)

Examples from medical handbooks:

> If a man continually has vertigo, his feet are limp, he suffers
> pains and he is repeatedly scared: 'Hand of Mankind' lies upon
> him. Silver, gold, bronze, iron, *anzahhu*-glass, white ditto,
> black ditto, (and) *zalāqu* (i.e. a bright stone).
> (The stones are probably to be worn in a leather bag. *BAM* III
> no. 317 rev. 24–6)

> If a man is bewitched: In a kettle you boil a potsherd of the
> river together with bitumen, put it in first-rate beer and take it
> on the last day of the month (i.e. the day of the disappearance
> of the moon), facing the sunrise you speak as follows: 'Sorcer-
> ess, your charms will turn back against you and seize you!' He
> shall say thus and he will get well.
> (*AMT* no. 85, 1 V 10–14)

> If a man's enemy has surrounded him with hate, *zikurudû*,
> perversion of justice, aphasia and evil magic and caused him to
> be in bad repute before god, king, lord and prince and his eyes

are afflicted. In order to dispel the evil magic: (Here follows a list of herbs that are mixed with magnetite and seven aromatic oils, then the prescription goes on:) You recite the incantation 'I am pleasing' three times over it and rub him with it and he will recover.
(*BAM* V no. 434 VI 1–11)

The Sumerian charm 'I am pleasing', was often recited over medicine against witchcraft. The way the speaker tries to confirm that he has a 'pleasing' character illustrates one of the assumed consequences of sorcery – divine wrath and conflicts with other persons, especially one's superiors. The incantation seems to have been rather popular and copies are known from Aššur, Nineveh and Sultantepe:

Incantation: I am pleasing, I am pleasing,
Heaven takes pleasure in me,
Šamaš, my god, takes pleasure in me,
The gods take pleasure in me,
The king takes pleasure in me,
The prince takes pleasure in me
The lord takes pleasure in me (variant adds: the judge takes pleasure in me, my judge takes pleasure in me, the judges take pleasure in me),
Man takes pleasure in me,
Mankind takes pleasure in me. May destiny be . . . (?),
May [the evil magic] be dispelled! Incantation formula.
(Nineveh: *BAM* V no. 434 VI 17–27; Aššur: *BAM* III no. 315 III 28–31; Sultantepe: *STT* I no. 19 II 26–33)

Medicine against *zikurudû* was, apparently, not much different; there is a remarkable sequence of recipes, known from at least four copies, making use of heads of birds, namely, goose, quail and eagle:

In order that *zikurudû* shall not approach a man: You dry the head of a goose and *imhur-limu* plant, you pound it (and) mix

it with fine oil, you rub him (with this) regularly and *zikurudû*
will not approach him and this man will be very old.
(*BAM* V no. 461 III 25'–28'; no. 463 rev. 1–3; no. 473 I
20–1; *BAM* III no. 209 obv. 28–30)

The Exorcist's Rituals against Witchcraft

Whereas the physician made use of medications in order to
alleviate physical and psychic symptoms, in cases of witchcraft the
exorcist performed a ritual with the purpose of restoring the
harmony between the bewitched person and the divine sphere
and freeing him from any impurity. Such impurity was conceived
of both in a concrete sense, as contact with something unclean
and, in a figurative sense, as the committing of a sin. The rituals,
therefore, had to be carried out in a pure place and sweeping the
ground and sprinkling with holy water usually began the ritual
actions. Then offerings were presented to one or more gods,
incense was burnt, and the god was finally addressed in a prayer
said by the bewitched person, or by the exorcist speaking for
him, explaining his situation, confessing his sins and ending with
a plea for purification and restoration of health and former
position. This procedure is similar to most other rituals, whether
they are against ghosts, demons or diseases or in order to avert
evil portents. However, in the case of witchcraft, the ritual is also
directed against the evildoer and the prayer contains as well an
appeal to the gods that they shall destroy the witches by turning
the evil magic against them. In order to make this purpose plain,
figurines of the witches are treated in the same way as the gods
are asked to treat them, by burning, dissolving in water, etc. As
already stated, the conjectured methods of witchcraft and those
prescribed in anti-witchcraft rituals are, it seems, identical. The
principle is apparently exactly that – that witchcraft has to be
counteracted by its own methods. If, for instance, certain symptoms have been diagnosed as sorcery due to figurines which have
been laid in a grave, a ritual with figurines is recommended to
dispel the evil magic. In a Maqlû incantation the actions of the
witches are described as follows: 'They have bewitched, they

have bewitched again and again, in order to roll me up like a mat, to clamp down upon me like a bird trap, to destroy me like a cliff, to cover me like a net'. Then the same actions are turned against the witches: 'But I – on the command of Marduk, the lord of the evening, (and on the command) of Asalluhi, the lord of exorcism – I will roll my sorcerer and my sorceress up like a mat, I will clamp down upon them like a bird trap, I will destroy them like a cliff, I will cover them like a net' (Maqlû II 160–80, see Meier, 1937: 19). According to its methods 'Black Magic' is therefore not to be separated from 'White Magic'; only its target and intentions distinguish illegal magic from the legal, healing ritual. An anti-witchcraft ritual is, therefore, by its very nature also evil magic, since it aims at injuring another person, this action being justified by the assumption that the other person, the witch, was the first to resort to such evil. But who is the guilty party, and who the innocent victim? In a way the anti-witchcraft rituals are really black magic. These quotations from prayers in the anti-witchcraft ritual Maqlû, demonstrate how the witch was to be treated:

> May they (the witches) die and I live,
> May they be expelled and I get well,
> May they perish and I prosper,
> May they be weak and I be strong.
> (Maqlû II 93–6, see Meier, 1937: 16)

> I will scatter your witchcraft, I will turn your words in your
>   mouth,
> May the evil magic you practised be against yourself,
> May the figurines you made represent yourself.
> (Maqlû V 5–7, see Meier, 1937: 34)

> Your sorcery, your evil magic, your witchcraft,
> The result of your witchcraft,
> Ea, the exorcist of the gods, has dissolved them,
> May your evil mouth be filled with dust,
> May your evil tongue be tied with strings,

At the command of Enbilulu, lord of life!
(Maqlû VII 106–11, see Meier, 1937: 50)[1]*

Only the gods knew who was guilty and who was innocent, and it is noticeable that several prayers are framed like speeches for the defence, with a god, mostly Šamaš, acting as the judge. The ritual replaced the legal trial which, as we have seen, probably rarely took place, either because the identity of the witch was not known, or because it was feared that the question of guilt could not be proved (see above, Laws against Witchcraft). In a trial, however, both parties, the accuser and the accused, must appear before the judges and in the prayers, therefore, the adversary, the witch, was represented by a figurine:

> Šamaš, these are my sorcerers (. . .), these are they who have
>   performed evil magic against me (. . .),
> [Šamaš], these are they, these are their figurines,
> [Since they are] not present, I have made figurines of them
>   and [I hold them] before [your great] divinity.
> They have afflicted me with witchcraft, sorceries, evil magic.
> (Here follows a long catalogue of the evil deeds of the
>   witches.)
> Šamaš, as to my sorcerer and sor[ceress], (. . .)
> May Girru, the burner, burn them!
> (Lambert 1957–8: 289–93, lines 1, 9–11, 54–9)

The idea of the ritual as a kind of trial, is already found in the first prayer of Maqlû, addressed to the gods of the night:

> Stand by me, great gods, listen to my plea!
> Decide my case, learn about my behaviour!
> I have made figurines of my sorcerer and sorceress,
> Placed them at your feet and (now) I plead the case.
> (Maqlû I 13–17, see Meier, 1937: 7)

The fire god, Girru, is also addressed in the rituals as the judge who convicts the witches by burning their images:

* Notes on pp. 151–2

Powerful Girru, raging storm,
You lead gods and kings aright,
You judge the case of the oppressed, male or female,
Stand by me in my process, like Šamaš, the hero,
Render judgment for me, give a decision for me,
Burn my sorcerer and my sorceress,
Eat my enemies, consume those who are evil to me!
(Maqlû II 126–32, see Meier, 1937: 17–18)

Another method of turning the evil magic against the witch is when a person washes himself over the figurines, as in the following apotropaic ritual. The water should transfer evil and impurities to the person represented by the image, while the purpose of pouring fish oil on the figurine, an action frequently prescribed in the rituals, was probably to pollute the adversary:

That witchcraft, sorcery, evil magic, (and) evil spells, whether of a man or a woman, may not approach a man: You make two figurines of clay, two of dough, two of wax, two of tallow, each pair male and female, and their names you write on their left shoulder; you turn their hands on their back, you bind their feet. Before Šamaš you place a censer (with) juniper; before Šamaš you say as follows:

Incantation: Šamaš, judge of heaven and earth, judge of
    above and below,
You, who guide the black-headed, set the prisoners free,
    revive the dead!
Šamaš, these are the figurines of my enemy, of my
    persecutor,
Of my adversary who has laid(?) upon me witchcraft,
    rebellion, hate,
'Cutting of the throat', perversion of justice, aphasia(?),
    everything evil (and) evil magic.
Šamaš, before your great divinity, let their 'cutting of the
    throat' (and) their witchcraft be in their (own) bodies.

When you have said this, you take the combings from their heads (and) clothe them (the figurines) in the combings; you bind them together with a string, place them in a vessel (and) [pour] fish oil over them [. . .]. You swing censer and torch over him (the man for whom the ritual is performed) (and) pour holy water over him. You bury them (the figurines) in the ground. From the first day of the month until the first day of the next month he shall wash himself over them and witchcraft, sorcery, evil magic (and) evil spells will return to the sorcerer and the sorceress (and) not approach that man. (Caplice, 1970: 135–9)

Maqlû

Burying or destroying the figurines of witches are characteristic of many anti-witchcraft rituals. The most complex ritual of this kind is rendered in the series Maqlû which means 'Burning' and refers to the burning of several images representing witches, enemies, wizards and evildoers of any kind, male or female. It took place during the night and was concluded at sunrise. The complex character of Maqlû alone shows that it could not have been carried out for people in general, and that it was in fact performed for the king is confirmed by a letter to Esarhaddon from one of his exorcists: 'In the evening the king will perform the Maqlû ritual, in the morning the king will perform the rest of the ritual' (*ABL* no. 56, cf. Parpola, 1970: 154–5 no. 208).

Maqlû is reconstructed primarily from numerous Neo-Assyrian copies from Nineveh and Aššur and also from a number of tablets from Babylonia, also found in the royal library in Nineveh. To these can now be added duplicates from Uruk dating from the Seleucid period. (The best edition of Maqlû is Meier, 1937; for the history and performance of the ritual, see Abusch, 1974 and 1989.)

Maqlû contains nearly 100 incantations or prayers, inscribed on eight clay tablets. The ninth and last tablet of the series is the so-called 'ritual tablet'. However, in this case, the ritual tablet does not contain real instructions, let alone a description of the ritual actions. Rather, it is a catalogue quoting the first line of the incantations in the same order as they occur on tablets one to eight, provided with very brief comments about the corresponding actions, e.g.: 'Incantation: "Girra, the Noble One, the First Son of Heaven", a figurine of bitumen' (Maqlû IX 33, see Meier, 1937: 58). From the ritual tablets and descriptions of the actions in the incantations, and by comparison with parallel texts, the content of Maqlû ritual can be rendered as follows:

Preparations in the Night: The ritual begins at night with a prayer to the stars, the gods of the night. Water and a plant called *maštakal* is used for purifying the place or the bewitched, i.e. the king, who also legitimizes himself. He is the messenger of the god Asalluhi and acts at his command. The evil actions of the witches are described and the bewitched prays for justice. The torch is lit and Nusku, fire god and god of the lamp, is praised.

Presentation of Figurines: Images of the witches are presented to the gods, especially to the fire god, Girru, who is to destroy them. They are made of various materials (tallow, clay, bitumen, dough, residue of linseed, wax, bitumen mixed with sulphur, tamarisk and cedar wood) and treated in different ways; for instance, a clay figurine has a peg in the back, and another is sealed with a cylinder seal. Moreover, figurines are placed in a boat of clay to be sent away on the river, and a potsherd from a crossroad is presented, symbolizing a thorn, a scorpion's sting and a steep mountain, beyond the reach of the witches. Most of these materials and treatments of the figurines are paralleled in other rituals against witchcraft outside the Maqlû series, but in no other ritual are so many figurines included as here. The incantations following each presentation enumerate like a catalogue all the evil deeds that the witch might have done and mostly end with a request to the fire God to burn the figurines and dissolve the evil machinations of the witches.

Dispelling of the Evil, Burning of Figurines: It is not mentioned exactly when the figurines are to be burnt, whether during the recitation of the corresponding incantation or at the end, or after all images have been presented. The burning also includes other objects – two reeds filled with blood and excrements and bound together as a cross, with a figurine fixed on each of the four ends, two cords of white wool, one with three knots, the other with seven, and fourteen potsherds representing seven pairs of witches, male and female. All are to be burnt in a kiln. Various plants are mentioned in the incantations that follow, probably because they were also thrown into the fire. Although these drugs are not those normally used for fumigations, they are otherwise known to be effective against witchcraft, like thyme. The others, as far as they can be identified, are sesame, colocynth(?), saffron(?), cress(?), mustard(?), and terebinth(?). After the burning the fire is extinguished with water: 'You calm down (the fire) with water'; with this action the anger of the witches is calmed down and the witchcraft deprived of its effect. Finally, a stone is laid upon the remnants.

Carrying away of the materia magica: What now follow, according to the ritual tablet, are actions also known, with some variations, in other contexts and probably characteristic of the ending of a ritual. The quoted incantations are not, however, included in the corresponding tablet of the series Maqlû, but partly known from other sources. The objects used in the ritual are brought out of the house to the accompanyment of the recitation of a Sumerian incantation with the incipit: 'Evil demon – to your plain'. On reaching the gate the exorcist scatters flour, then he returns and enters the house.

Fumigation and apotropaic actions: For purification of the house, especially the bed chamber, apotropaic images are placed at the doors, incense is burned at the head of the bed (which has been surrounded by a multi-coloured cord), and thereafter the patient is also cleansed by fumigation. Several plants, sulphur and salt are laid on the censer, and for each of these objects a short incantation has to be recited. This part of the ritual also aims at preventing the evil entering the house anew; flour and beer is offered and the doorjambs smeared with oil. The text is fragmentary here, but the bed is probably surrounded by a circle of flour and this section of the ritual is concluded by the recitation of two incantations praying that evil should be far from the house.

Purification in the morning: The patient washes his hands over images of the witches placed in a washbowl, and then whips the water three times with a twig of ash wood. The hand wash is repeated several times over various images, probably of water-soluble materials like dough, and accompanied by several incantations describing the acts of the witches. All this illustrates that the evil is transferred to the witches, dissolved and undone. During the washing the morning and the sun god are praised. At last the ritual tablet gives some details for the exorcist: 'You throw chaff in a pot and blow it through the opening (of the pot) into a washbowl'; 'you make a clay figurine of the sorceress and place a stone on her breast, he (the patient) should wash his hands over it and strike it three times with a piece of ash wood'; 'you make two breads and images of the sorcerer and the sorceress, you put them (the images) into(?) the breads; you lift the breads to the right and left of the patient and recite the incantation, then you give them to a dog and a bitch (to eat).' At last the water is brought away and poured out while the exorcist recites, among others, the incantation 'I hold my curved staff', declaring that the bewitched has been released.

Zikurudû

Counteractions against *zikurudû*, 'cutting the throat', are totally different. In these cases the evil magic is dispelled not by destroying images, but through manipulations of the objects used for this type of witchcraft – notably a small animal, for instance a kind of mouse or a mongoose. Further, the rituals are usually performed at night before a star – the Great Bear, the Arrow star (i.e. Sirius), Scorpio or the full moon – apparently the same stars and deities before whom the evil magic has been carried out (see above, Messages of Witchcraft and Thomsen, 1987: 40–7). Only a small number of instructions against *zikurudû* is known so far, almost exclusively from Neo-Assyrian Nineveh, and many of them are fragmentary. According to a letter from one of the exorcists of the Assyrian king, a ritual was performed for a prince: '[Wh]at the king, my lord, wrote to me [about] Šarrat-samsī, to perform the ritual against *zikurudû* for him we again pronounced (his) name (and) performed (it). We are not negligent with regard to the work and rituals (but) perform (them) regularly' (*ABL* no. 636, see Parpola, 1970: 118–19, no. 157)

Besides the rituals there are also medical prescriptions for ointments and potions against *zikurudû*. For instance, five stones or minerals, among them pieces of glass of different colours, iron and magnetite, are crushed and mixed with cypress oil, an oil often used against witchcraft. The mixture stands overnight 'under the stars' and at sunrise the whole body is rubbed with this oil. Further, the bewitched person should look upon red gold and step upon bitumen in order to get rid of the sorcery (*BAM* V no. 449 III 5'–7').

In a serious case of *zikurudû* – it is prognosticated that the patient will die within ten days – the ritual prescribes the construction of a reed hut. At night a reed hut is erected on the roof, most likely before the Great Bear in front of which the evil magic is assumed to have been performed. Standards are set up in the four directions of the winds, the exorcist sprinkles with holy water and draws a circle of flour, and inside the reed hut standards are decorated with red and blue(?) wool. After this the patient is apparently led into the reed hut, but the tablet is broken here and the rest of the ritual instructions are lost (*AMT* No. 44, 4: 4–9). A reed hut is also mentioned in another, unfortunately fragmentary, ritual against *zikurudû* (PBS 1/2 no. 121) and in a few purification rituals.

A purification, very similar to an apotropaic ritual, is prescribed to take place before Sirius, called the 'arrow star' and identified with the warrior god Ninurta:

Before the Arrow star you sweep the roof (and) sprinkle pure water; you scatter juniper in the censer on thornwood coals, you libate beer, you kneel, you draw a curtain, you heap up flour. You purify this man with censer and torch and holy water and between the curtain you let him stand on garden plants and let him lift his hands. You recite this incantation three times, while you recite (this) he shall kneel and (then) speak everything which occupies his mind and the wrath of his god and goddess will be dissolved, the evil magic which was made will be dissolved.

(*BAM* V no. 461 III 5'–13'; no. 462, 3'–10'; for the prayer to Sirius/Ninurta see Mayer, 1976: 540–1: Kaksisa 3)

In the cases where it is explicitly said that the *zikurudû* magic has manifested itself by the appearance of a certain kind of mouse (*arrabu*) or a mongoose, the animal is somehow treated in the ritual, as in the following instructions of which the beginning as well as the prayer to Sin are broken off. The ritual is performed before the full moon and funeral rites are celebrated for the *arrabu* mouse, with gifts and offerings to the gods of the Nether World, in order that it remains there and does not return to earth to threaten the man anew:

'Dissolve the (magic) knots that are surrounding me!' You let him recite this before Sin seven times and let him bow down. He should make his food offering to Sin in the same night; on the fifteenth day (of the month) to Sin he should say everything which occupies his mind. Let him pray every day.

You take the *arrabu* mouse and put it in a mouse skin, in this (skin) you (also) put pieces of silver, gold, iron, lapis lazuli, *dušû* (and) *nirpappardillû* stone, oil, oil of first quality, *igulû*-oil, oil of cedar, honey, butter, milk, wine and vinegar you pour into it, you tie up the face and cover it with a linen cloth, you gather it in a grave (and) perform the funeral rites. You praise it (the *arrabu*) pay respect to it and perform the rites until the seventh day; then the *zikurudû* magic which was made against this man will never approach him as long as he lives.

(*BAM* V no. 449 II 1–10. For this text and funeral rites in magic rituals in general see Tsukimoto, 1985, 125–45)

In cases where the animal was thrown away, perhaps before its significance was realized, the exorcist also knew an appropriate remedy; the man was to bring his offerings before the full moon, bow down and tell all his worries, and the evil magic would not approach him (*BAM* V no. 449 II 11–15).

MAGIC

Luck and Misfortune

In everyday life the first rule for avoiding evil was to observe the standards of moral behaviour; respect the gods, be honest and righteous, and behave well towards the poor and the weak. Moreover, one had to keep away from everything unclean, even not touching something which had been handled by an impure person, or speaking with a man who had committed a sin, or eating such a person's food. Otherwise one became impure and was punished by divine wrath, manifesting itself as bad luck, misfortune and even serious illness. Other offences interfering with the relations between man and god were, for instance, eating certain things on certain days of the month and making a mistake when praying or bringing offerings to a god. An oath was often feared to bring evil upon the one who swore it. A person might not know exactly what he had done wrong and in such a case a ritual called Šurpu, 'Burning', would cleanse him and release him from his sins, whatever they were (for an edition of Šurpu see Reiner, 1958). During this ceremony prayers with lengthy catalogues of possible offences against moral rules, taboos etc. were recited, asking the gods to reveal the specific reason for the disease and the misfortune of the patient and to undo it. The purification was performed as an act of sympathetic magic; an onion was peeled and burnt, dates were stripped off and burnt, a fleece of wool was plucked apart and burnt, and so on. A similar ritual was carried out in a reed hut and addressed to the personal gods of the patient, as the first line of the prayer demonstrates: 'My god, I do not know (my sin)' (this was also the name of this ritual). The purification was also made by burning various objects and figurines and by sprinkling with water (for an edition of this ritual see Ebeling, 1931b: 114–20).

In addition, certain days were thought to be unfavourable, either for any actions or for specific actions which should either not be done at all on such days or done only after performing certain apotropaic actions. These rules were collected in hemerologies – exhaustive catalogues of favourable and unfavourable days for every month of the year and lists of positive or negative actions for each month. These texts show that certain months or days of the month were generally favourable, others unfavourable. In still other cases, whether an action was to be recommended or not depended on the circumstances. Some of these rules were certainly common knowledge, others were collected by exorcists, diviners and other scholars from old and rare sources in order to gain as much information as possible for their important task of protecting the king and his family. The hemerological tradition goes back at least to the second millennium BC but most texts are Neo-Assyrian or later. One of them predicts the consequences of certain actions in each month of the year; e.g.: 'If a man builds a house in the month of Nisan: the foundations will not be secure; if (he builds it) in Ajar he will experience grief; if (he builds it) in Siman: he will rejoice', and so on (Labat, 1965: 62–3 §5 l. 1–3; for hemerologies in general see Labat, 1975).

The magic texts offer several remedies against bad luck, worries, everyday annoyance and the like. For instance, in a recipe against all kinds of bad luck caused by witchcraft nine drugs, among them mandrake(?), coral, tamarisk and thornbush, are put into a leather bag, two incantations are recited over this, and it is then worn around the neck. The text then states: 'The (personal) god and goddess of this man will bless him; his mood will become all right; his dreams will be pleasant; whatever he says will find acceptance; god, king, influential person and nobleman will stand by him; whenever he goes to court, the judgment will be favourable for him' (*BAM* III no. 316 II 22'–5'). In order to avoid evil in general or, for example, to appear pleasant to his adversaries or masters a person could wear an amulet (a stone, a ring, a string of wool), or he could rub himself with oil containing aromatic plants.

A collection of such instructions, especially for attracting the goodwill of the king, and thus probably also especially important for the scholars of the king, is called 'Entering the palace'. The incantations are short and the instructions not especially complicated, as in the following for which the incantation is broken off:

> You recite the incantation over the *kapāsu* shell and tie it into your hem. You enter before the prince and the king will be friendly to you.
> (*KAR* no. 238 (= VAT 8014) rev. 6–7, see Ebeling, 1931a: 41–2)

The formulations of the next incantation are close to those of anti-witchcraft texts:

> [Beginning broken]
> You of heaven, pay attention,
> You of earth, listen to my words!
> Until I smite the cheek of my adversary NN, son of NN,
> (Until) I pull out his tongue,
> turn his word into his mouth,
> (Until) his mouth revolts against talking,
> I will not recite the incantation for . . .

Incantation for entering the palace. You recite the incantation three times over a copper ring and put it on your finger. You enter before the prince and he will be friendly to you.
(*KAR* no. 71 rev. 1–11, see Ebeling, 1931a: 32 and 34)

Anointing the face and hands with oil of some kind is very often prescribed in these texts:

> Incantation: I rub myself with oil of power(?), my hands are full of oil of handcuffs!

Towards god, king, master, prince (and) noblemen my
   head is held high!
To the presence of my lord I will bring seven young girls.

Its ritual: You recite this incantation three times over fine oil
and rub your face and hands with it, and you enter before the
prince and he will be friendly to you.
(*KAR* no. 237, 13–17 and *LKA* no. 105, 1–5 see Ebeling,
1931a: 37–8 and 40)

A similar instruction is 'to calm anger', where the incantation
indicates that the man speaking is involved in a lawsuit:

> They have brought me to court in a difficult case . . .
> Because of a contract at the Palace Gate,
> Because of the assembly of the masters.
> Ninkarrak,[2] seize your young dogs!
> Put muzzles on the mouths of your strong dogs!
> Tall one, be silent, short one, speak not!
> Nobody sees you.
> I am wearing an *ashar*-stone,[3] the *ashar*-stone [. . .]
> May it make my adversary in court change his
>   opinion [. . .].

It is an incantation to calm anger. Its ritual: You recite this
incantation three times over an *ashar*-stone. You place it on his
neck, you rub him with oil and he will get well.
(*KAR* no. 71, 1–13 and *LKA* no. 104 obv. 12-rev. 2, see
Ebeling, 1931a: 30–1 and 33)

The Power of Precious Stones

It was a common belief that, like herbs in medicine, stones and
minerals (worn on the body in a necklace or in a leather bag) had
positive effects against attack by diseases and demons and in many
other situations. Among the scholarly handbooks there are both
systematic lists of stones describing their appearance and qualities
(see Horowitz, 1992) and numerous prescriptions for composing
such necklaces for various purposes – for instance, against the

anger of specific gods, bad omens, ghosts, fear and diseases, to undo witchcraft, or in order that the god should take pity on a man. But there are also stones 'for joy', 'for profit and abundance', and 'for being (or making) favourable'. It seems that the combination of several sorts of stones was thought especially effective, since many stones and minerals like gold, silver, jasper, lapis lazuli, cornelian and hematite occur very often in different contexts and it is difficult to say what the characteristic of each one was supposed to be. On the other hand, these were also stones which were rare or expensive, so there might have been occasions when not all the prescribed stones were available. Tradition associated such chains of stones with two great Babylonian kings; fourteen stones, among them lapis lazuli, jasper and green obsidian, were called the chain of Naram-Sin, the famous conqueror and king of the Akkadian Empire in the twenty-third century BC, while another chain was attributed to Hammurapi, king of Babylon (1792–1750). No specific purpose for these chains is mentioned, but, given their supposed age and the celebrity of the named kings, an all-round favourable effect was presumably ascribed to them.

As to the method for preparing or consecrating the stones and producing the necklace there is little information. Apparently they were simply strung on a woollen thread or put into a small leather bag and worn around the neck for some time, until the patient was cured or the danger was considered to be over. Stones were also used in this way after the performance of healing and apotropaic rituals in order to confirm their effect. For example, in a ritual for dispelling the evil and death that have befallen a man and his family ten stones were placed in water together with plants and substances typically used in water for purifications (tamarisk, cedar, salt and others). After the ritual was finished, they were placed around the neck of the man. Similarly, after an apotropaic ritual against evil portended by a malformed newborn animal, the man affected by this omen had to wear a necklace with stones for seven days (*AMT* No. 71, 1, see Ebeling, 1955a: 170–1 and 176–7; Caplice, 1965: 125–9). There are also prescriptions for tying stones to different parts of the body, mostly the forehead, neck, right and left arm and hand, the waist and the right and left leg, for such purposes as help for 'a woman who does not give birth easily' (*STT* II no. 241).

Amulets

The stones for necklaces were most probably simply beads or small pieces which of course could have been polished or formed into a certain shape. It was not the form, however, but the qualities of the stone that were important. Otherwise, amulets were small objects of stone or bronze, for instance statuettes of the four-winged demon Pazuzu, or heads of this demon, and plaques with representations of Pazuzu and the female demon Lamaštu, mostly inscribed with short incantations. A band of lead to be worn around the neck on a string of blue wool would 'loosen' or 'open' the hand, which probably means that other persons, especially superiors, would be benevolent and generous to the person wearing it (*KAR* no. 238 rev. 8'-18' see Ebeling, 1931a: 41–3). These objects were perforated so that they could be worn in a necklace or – in the case of bigger objects – hung on the wall, at the bedside or elsewhere. This was probably also the purpose of tablets in amulet shape, i.e. having a projection at the top which was pierced through horizontally and inscribed with, for instance, an excerpt from the Epic of Erra, such as a praise of Erra, god of death and plague, and apparently intended to save the house where it was hung up. Other tablets of the same shape were inscribed with prayers to Ea, Šamaš and Marduk, and even a hemerological text. (For such tablets see Reiner, 1960b.)

A tablet of amulet shape, and therefore certainly meant to be hung up in a house, is inscribed with incantations and instructions for three rituals: (a) 'that brisk trading should not forget the house of innkeeper, diviner, physician, exorcist or cook'; (b) 'if an innkeeper's income has ceased'; and (c), quoted below, 'for the profit of an innkeeper on the quay'. In all three cases the goddess Ištar is invoked. The text is preserved in two copies, one found

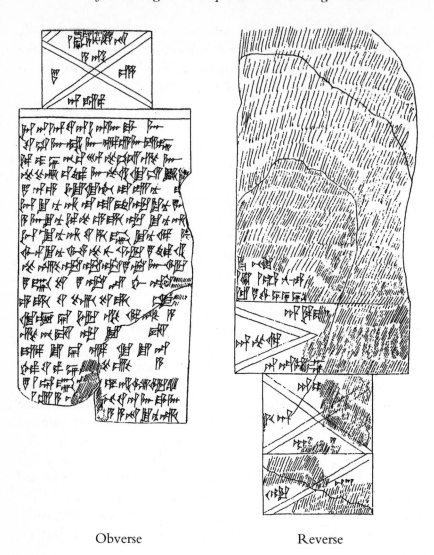

Obverse   Reverse

Figure 1: Copy of a clay tablet of amulet shape, Assur 7th century BC (*KAR* no. 35).

The obverse is inscribed with a prayer to Ea, Šamaš and Marduk asking for protection against witchcraft. Four fields with diagonal lines contain an invocation of Marduk and Išum with a plea for guarding the house of the person named in the field on the top of the obverse.

Figure 2: The demon Pazuzu. Bronze statuette, Assyrian, first half of the 1st millennium BC (Musée du Louvre)

Figurines and heads of Pazuzu were worn as amulets; bigger examplars were probably placed in the house to protect against diseases.

Figure 3: Bronze amulet, Assyrian, 8th–7th century BC (Musée du Louvre)

At the top the head of the demon Pazuzu whose body is shown on the reverse. On the obverse in the first field the attributes of the great gods; beneath them seven evil demons with animal heads; in the third field a person is lying in a bed surrounded by protective deities. At the bottom left the demon Pazuzu, in the middle the female demon Lamaštu with a dog and a piglet sucking her breasts, to the right her attributes often mentioned in ritual texts (see Farber, 1987): spindle, comb, container(?), vessel, fibula, leg of a donkey, boot, sandal and fringed textile.

in the royal residence at Nineveh (K. 3464 = *ABRT* I pp. 66–7 and Lenormant, 1875 no. 99), the other in the Assyrian religious capital Aššur (*KAR* No. 144), which, according to its colophon, is copied from a text from Babylon; both texts are Neo-Assyrian (edition by Ebeling, 1955b: 178–84; translation by Caplice, 1974: 23–4).

> Incantation: Ištar of (all) lands, the most valiant of the
>   goddesses!
> This is your residence,[4] be joyous and exult!
> Come, enter our house! Your sweet bedfellow may enter
>   with you, your lover and your dancer(?) (may enter
>   with you)!
> Let my lips be *lallaru*-honey, let my hands be (sexual)
>   charm!
> Let the lips of my vulva(?) be honey!
> Like birds twitter when a snake comes out of its hole, let
>   people fight over me!
> From the residence of Ištar, from the storehouse of Ninlil,[5]
> From the herds of Ningišzidda,[6] seize him, bring him, be
>   friendly to him!
> Let the remote one return to me, let the angry one come
>   back to me. Let his heart return to me like smoke!
>
> Like heaven fertilizes the earth and makes plants abundant,
>   so let greetings to me be abundant!

An incantation for the profit of the innkeeper at the quay.

> Its ritual: dust from a quay, dust from a ferry, dust from a bridge, dust from a crossing of four roads, dust from a cross-roads, dust from a city gate, dust from a dais, dust from the door of the Ištar temple, dust from a prostitute's house, dust from the door of a gardener's house, dust from the door of a cook's house, dust from the door of an innkeeper's house whose profit is plentiful – (you take) all these (pieces of) dust. Before Ištar you erect a reed altar, you place three portions of breast-shaped breads, you set out a censer with juniper, you

libate beer, recite the incantation seven times and prostrate yourself. Those dusts you soften in water, you recite the incantation seven times (over the mixture) (and) wash the door of the house (with it); from the rest you make a figurine of an ox and bury it under a vat.

This incantation is a prayer to Ištar for help, apparently spoken by a woman, probably a prostitute of a tavern where the custom has dried up. To erect a reed altar and offer bread, beer or wine, and incense is the normal ritual practice. However, the collection of dust from many different places is specific to the rituals on this tablet, although the use of dust is known elsewhere too. The principle is clearly *similia similibus*; the places mentioned, like 'the door of the house of the prostitute', indicate the character of the business that it is hoped to increase, since the house of the innkeeper was a place of leisure, of drinking beer and wine, and also a place where contacts with prostitutes were made.

Amulets for the Protection of Babies

A prescription for producing an amulet to protect a baby from the attack of the evil *alû*-demon reads: '[You make] a cylinder of clay from the potter's pit and write the incantation upon it, you bake it in fire made of . . . You place it either on his neck or hang it at the head of his bed. Evil of any kind will not approach him' (K. 3628+ rev. 9–12, see Farber, 1989: 128–9). The incantation used in this case was frequently inscribed on amulets and invokes Sirius, i.e. the god Ninurta. Clay cylinders with this incantation have also been found.

A high number of amulets depict the female demon Lamaštu who afflicted babies and pregnant women. She has the head of a lion, ears of an ass, eagle's talons and occasionally wings. Some of these amulets are crude drawings with strokes and signs imitating cuneiform writing, while others are beautiful pieces of art showing not only the demon but also a bed with a person surrounded by protective spirits and gods and inscribed with an incantation telling that Ninurta has assigned the evil demons to the nether world. (For the demon Lamaštu and these amulets, see Farber, 1983.)

Love Charms

Lovemaking and sexual matters also concerned the exorcist and physician, as attested by several tablets with prescriptions for awakening the desire of a woman, for eliminating a rival and for potency problems. Whereas medications for sexual troubles, especially impotence, are found in high number, examples of love charms are rather few and they are always directed towards a woman with whom a man has fallen in love. The converse situation, when a woman wants to attract the attention of a man, has not so far been attested. Practices used by women in such cases might have belonged to an oral tradition, not likely to be included in the learned lore of the magical and medical experts. (For an edition and thorough study of these texts see Biggs, 1967.)

The earliest example from Mesopotamia of a love charm is from about 2200 BC. The text in the Old Akkadian language is difficult and frequent shifts of speaker impede the understanding, but the intention, to make a girl fall in love with a young man, is clear. The phraseology of the charm is closely related to love lyrics, comparable to those of the Song of Songs (edited by Westenholz, 1977). A similar, Sumerian incantation has survived in two copies, both from the beginning of the second millennium BC. There are no ritual instructions added but a remedy is described in the conjuration itself pretending to be the teaching of Enki to his son Asalluhi, a frequent motif in Sumerian incantations. The pair of lovers *par excellence* in Sumerian mythology and love lyric is Inanna (Akkadian: Ištar) and Dumuzi, which explains why the desired woman is compared with this goddess:

> The beautiful girl, standing in the street,
> The beautiful girl, the harlot, Inanna (var.: daughter of
>   Inanna), standing in the tavern,
> She is abundant butter, she is abundant cheese,

She is a cow, exalted woman, she is Inanna,
She is the lofty storehouse of Enki.
When the girl sits, she is a grove of apple trees rich of fruits,
When she lies down, . . ., she is a shadow-spreading cedar
  branch.
She stretches her limbs towards him – they are limbs of
  lovemaking!
She stretches her hands towards him – they are hands of
  lovemaking!
She stretches her eyes towards him – they are eyes of
  lovemaking!
She stretches her feet towards him – they are feet of
  lovemaking!
The pure threshold, the doorframe(?) of lapis lazuli,
When she descends, the threshold . . .
  . . . (two unintelligible lines)
Love, from heaven like dew . . .
Let the breast(?) of the young man . . . like a reed.
Asalluhi saw it,
He went to his father Enki in the temple and tells him:
'My father! The beautiful girl, standing in the street.'
As he has repeated (all this, he said:)
'What I shall do in this case, I do not know, how shall I
  cure him?'
Enki answered his son, Asalluhi:
'My son! What do you not know? What can I add to you?
Asalluhi, what do you not know? What can I add to you?
What I know, you know too!
Tallow from a pure cow, milk from a mother cow,
Tallow from a cow, tallow from a white cow
You pour into a green flask,
You put(?) it on the breast of the girl.'
The girl shall not lock the open door,
She shall not comfort her crying child,
(but instead) let her run after me!
(Falkenstein, 1964: 113–29.)

Although the early love charms demonstrate that this practice was part of an old tradition, most of the texts dealing with lovemaking and related matters are from the Neo-Assyrian period. A tablet which belonged to the library of the exorcist family in Aššur (seventh century BC) contains among others a Sumerian incantation to the same purpose and, therefore, perhaps of a much older date. On the tablet there are two more incantations 'for amusement', which is probably a synonym for lovemaking or love-play; in most cases the incantations and ritual actions are addressed to the goddess of love, Inanna/Ištar:

> Incantation: The beautiful woman has brought forth love.
> Inanna, who loves apples and pomegranates,
> Has brought forth potency.
> Rise! Fall! Love-stone, prove effective for me! Rise!
> . . . Inanna . . . (context unintelligible)
> She has presided over love.

> Incantation: If a woman looks upon the penis of a man.

Its ritual: You recite the incantation three times over an apple or a pomegranate. You give it to the woman (and) have her suck their juice. That woman will come to you (and) you can make love to her.[7]

If ditto: If that woman does not come, you take *tappinnu*-flour[8] (and) throw (it) into the river to King Ea; you take clay from banks of the two rivers, from the far side (of the Tigris) and the far side (of the Euphrates); you make a figurine of that woman, you write her name on its left shoulder. Facing Šamaš you recite the incantation: 'The Beautiful Woman' over it. At the outer gate of the West Gate you bury it . . . (text unintelligible) At midday(?) or . . . she will walk over it. You recite the incantation: 'The Beautiful Woman' three times (and) that woman will come to you (and) you can make love to her. (For this and similar texts see Biggs, 1967: 70–8)

Potency Incantations

Sexual problems, especially impotence, are the subject of a genre of magico-medical texts with a Sumerian title ŠÀ.ZI.GA, 'rising of the "heart" (i.e. the penis)', containing incantations, ritual instructions and recipes for medications (these texts are edited by Biggs, 1967). The prescriptions are possibly not solely for medical therapy but also meant simply to increase the joy and satisfaction of sex, for instance when the male and female sexual organs are rubbed with oil. The incantations are full of sexual metaphors and unambiguous invitations to be excited and get an erection; the mating of animals and the sexually excited ram and stallion are described, and the penis is compared to a harp string, a weapon or a stick. The choice of words alone is apparently aimed at stimulating the lovers. In some cases the incantation is unambiguously spoken by a woman, seeking to excite the man sexually and make him copulate with her. The therapy for impotence also frequently included both man and woman.

> [Incantation. At the] head of my bed a ram is tied.
> [At the foot of my bed] a weaned(?) sheep is tied. Around
>   my waist their wool is tied.
> [Like a ram eleven times,] like a weaned(?) sheep twelve
>   times, like a partridge(?) thirteen times
> [Make love to me, and like a] pig fourteen times, like a
>   wild bull fifty times, like a stag fifty times!
> (*KAR* no. 236 rev. 16–19 and *LKA* no. 99d I 26–30, see
>   Biggs, 1967: 30. The text is reconstructed from parallel
>   phrases in other potency incantations)

> Incantation. Let the wind blow, let the mountains quake!
> Let the clouds gather, let the rain fall!
> Let (the penis of) the ass become stiff, let him mount the
>   jenny!
> Let the he-goat get an erection, let him again and again
>   mount the young she-goat!

At the head of my bed a he-goat is tied (var.: I have
  indeed tied a he-goat)!
At the foot of my bed is a ram tied (var.: I have indeed
  tied a ram)!
The one at the head of my bed, get an erection, make
  love to me!
The one at the foot of my bed, get an erection, caress me!
My vagina is the vagina of a bitch! His penis is the penis
  of a dog!
As the vagina of a bitch holds fast the penis of a dog, (so
  may my vagina hold fast his penis)!
May your penis become as long as a *mašgašu*![9]
I sit in a web of laughter,
May I not miss the prey! Incantation formula.

Incantation for potency.
(*KAR* no. 236, 1–14 = no. 70 rev. 10–21 = no. 243 obv.(!)
1–11, see Biggs, 1967: 32–3)

Therapy
Most of the prescriptions are rather short medical recipes for a
potion or a mixture of herbs and oil for rubbing the penis and
vagina. The principle of the therapeutic methods is *similia similibus*. Parts of sexually excited animals or those animals which are
considered remarkably active in sexual relations, like bulls, rams,
stags and certain birds, especially the partridge(?), are made the
ingredients of potions and ointments or are worn on the body as
amulets. Remarkably often crushed magnetite and iron are used
for ointments. These minerals are very common in Babylonian
medicine, but they are obviously used here as well because of
their hardness.

To be effective a potency incantation was recited, usually seven
times, over the medications, as in the instructions for the incantation just quoted:

Its ritual: You put powder of magnetite (and) powder of iron
[into] *pūru*-oil; you recite the incantation over (it) seven times;

the man rubs his penis, the woman her vagina (with the oil),
then he can have inter[course].
(Biggs, 1967: 33, lines 15–17)

Other recipes stipulate, for instance, that the left(?) wing of a
bat should be dried and crushed, with three possibilities for its
use; it could be drunk with beer, mixed with oil for an ointment,
or worn around the neck in a leather bag (Biggs, 1967: 45 no.
26, lines 12'–14'). Parts of a bird called *issur hurri*, lit.: 'bird of a
hole', probably 'partridge', that was thought to be especially
active in sexual relations, were very popular in the potency
therapy; e.g.: 'the head of a male partridge(?), a silver bead, a gold
bead, the dewclaw of a stag you put into a leather bag' (*LKA* no.
103, 10–11 see Biggs, 1967: 26); or the man should swallow the
heart of a partridge(?), and at sunrise, while standing upon twigs
from a thornbush and facing the sun, he should drink a mixture
of water, the bird's blood, and spittle from a bull (*KAR* no. 70,
22–7 see Biggs, 1967: 26). Also interesting is the comparison of
the penis with the string of a lyre and the use of such a string in
the ritual: 'Let my penis be like a string of a lyre, that it will not
slip out of her!', and the ritual: 'You take the string of a lyre
(and) tie three knots, you recite the incantation seven times and
bind it on his right and left hands and he will have potency'
(*LKA* no. 101 rev. 12–19 and duplicates, see Biggs, 1967: 35).

    In the main, two reasons for impotence are mentioned in the
texts: witchcraft and the 'Hand of Ištar', i.e. punishment from
Ištar, goddess of lovemaking, for some offence against her and
her cult. To find out why the impotence has afflicted the man
there are instructions for an oracle; if a pig approaches figurines
of the man and woman it is the 'Hand of Ištar', and if it does not
approach it is witchcraft. In this case it was assumed that semen
from the man had been put in a grave.

Diseases and Demons
Judging from the comprehensive medical handbooks, a tradition
which goes back to the Old Babylonian period, the physician

observed and distinguished several symptoms and had a large repertory of recipes at his disposal to relieve the condition of the patient. Mainly herbal medications were used, but little can be said about their possible effect since only a few plant names have so far been identified. Both the production and the application of the medicine was often accompanied by magical actions like the recitation of incantations, and in addition the collection of the herbs from certain places or at a certain time of the day could be prescribed. If the condition of the patient was serious or the illness had lasted long and he was not getting better, the competence of the exorcist was required (for the physician versus the exorcist, see Ritter, 1965). Diseases were diagnosed as the effects of either various demons, a ghost, witchcraft or an angry god. The real cause for this misery was impurity or some offence which the patient had committed, whereupon the gods, especially the personal god or goddess, had withdrawn their protection. For the success of the cure it was important to know the exact nature of the illness, which was established by examining the physical symptoms as described in the diagnostic handbook of the exorcist (see Labat, 1951). Sometimes an oracle could give the answer, as in the case above where figurines were presented to a pig and its attitudes decided whether the impotence was due to witchcraft or the 'Hand of Ištar'. The purpose of the various rituals employed by the exorcist was both to purify the patient, thus freeing him from the impurity and sin he might have committed, and to restore the relations between him and the gods. Moreover, the demon (or ghost) had to be expelled or the sorcery undone. This was often practised as an act of sympathetic magic by burning or burying images of the evil, while another method was to offer a substitute for the patient.

Expelling Demons by Offering a Substitute

Sumerian incantations against evil demons describe how an animal, usually a goat or a pig, was offered as a substitute for the sick person. The purpose of the ritual was the transference of the disease or demon from the man to the animal. The goat or pig was slaughtered and cut into pieces, each limb was declared the limb of the patient, and the demon was conjured to leave him and take possession of the animal instead. Such incantations with Akkadian translations have survived in copies from the first millennium BC but it is highly probable that the tradition goes back to the beginning of the second millennium or even earlier. The descriptions are in a poetic language and give only a few practical instructions for the exorcist. Many questions as to how the ritual was carried out are thus left unanswered. Although the incantations were copied in the Neo-Assyrian period there is no information about whether they were in fact recited during such performances.

> Enki, the great prince, lord of incantations,
> To the Enki gods and the Ninki gods[10]
> Has given the he-goat as (the patient's) counterpart,
> He has invoked the sage,
> The kid (as) substitute for the man,
> The kid he has given for his (the patient's) life,
> He has given the head of the kid for the head of the man,
> He has given the neck of the kid for the neck of the man,
> He has given the breast of the kid for the breast of the man,
> He has given the right 'arm' of the kid for the right arm of
>   the man,
> He has given the left 'arm' of the kid for the left arm of the
>   man,
> He has given the blood of the kid for the blood of the man,
> He has given the heart of the kid for the heart of the man,
> (The text goes on naming other parts of the body and
>   ends:)
> The incantation (thus) spoken is the word of Enki,
> [. . .] May it not be undone!
> (*CT* 17 pl. 6 III 37–43 and pl. 37 Tablet 'Z' col. B, *STT* II
>   no. 172, 7–43; cf. Thompson, 1904: 21–3)

In these incantations the ritual is mostly rendered as the direct instructions of Enki, god of magic, to his son Asalluhi, the divine exorcist, who has seen and felt pity for the sick man:

[Take] a piglet [. . .],
[Place it] at the head of the patient,
Tear out its heart (and)
[Put it] on the upper part of the body of the patient,
[Sprinkle] its blood around his bed,
Dismember the piglet to correspond to his limbs,
Spread them (the limbs of the piglet) on the sick man,
Purify (and) cleanse
This man with holy water from the pure Abzu,
Move the censer and torch past him,
Twice you sling seven loaves baked in embers against the
    outer door,
Give the piglet as his substitute,
Give the flesh for his flesh, the blood for his blood – May
    (the demon) accept it!
The heart which you placed on his heart, you offer
    instead of his heart – May (the demon) accept it!
(*CT* 17 pl. 5–6: II 43 – III 18, for a translation of the
    whole text see Thompson, 1904: 13–25)

In the next example Enki is also speaking, instructing his son
Asalluhi to take a white kid as a substitute for the patient, then:

Place it near the patient,
Tear out its heart,
Put it in the hands of the man,
Recite the incantation of Eridu,[11]
Remove the heart of the kid (and) rub that man with bread
and dough,
Move the censer and torch past him,
Throw it (bread and dough) into the street,
Draw a circle of flour around that man,
Recite the incantation of Eridu (and) adjure them (the demons)
by the great gods:
The evil *udug*, the evil *ala*, the evil ghost,
Lamaštu, *labasu*,
Asakku, the grievous fate which are in the body of the man,

Be removed! Leave the house!
May the good *udug* (and) the good *lamma* be present!
The evil *udug*, the evil *ala*, the evil ghost,
Lamaštu, *labasu*,
the disease of the heart . . . headache, toothache,
Asakku, grievous fate
Be conjured by Heaven and Earth![12]
(*CT* 17 pl. 10–11: 73–103, for a translation see Thompson,
1904: 33–7)

The text is called an incantation for *máš hul dúb-ba*, a Sumerian
term of which the meaning is unclear, perhaps 'kid which makes
the evil tremble' or 'which beats (i.e. averts) the evil'. A
ceremony using a *máš hul dúb-ba* is sometimes mentioned in ritual
instructions from the Neo-Assyrian period and later, and then
apparently as a purification of the house. Censer and torch are
moved around and a circle of flour is drawn at the gate; a bell
and a drum are also used in some cases to drive away the demons.

A substitute ritual in which a kid is given to Ereškigal, queen
of the nether world, as a substitute for a sick man, is known from
two copies, both found in Aššur and dating from the seventh
century BC. The actions imitate the death and funeral of the
patient by slaughtering and burying the kid. The text does not
specify the situation in which it was required to present a
substitute to Ereškigal; possibly it was a serious disease which was
assumed to have a fatal end, or a case of witchcraft. Before the
ritual begins a grave is dug in the house and the kid is placed in
the bed of the patient where it must lie during the night. Before
dawn(?) the exorcist places the man and the kid on the ground in
the room where the grave has been made:

You touch the throat of the patient with a knife of tamarisk
wood, you cut the throat of the goat with a knife of bronze,
you wash the insides of the dead (goat) with water and anoint
it with oil, you fill its insides with aromatic plants, you provide
it with a garment and put shoes on it, you smear its eyes with
antimony, you put fine oil on its head, you take off the sick

man's headband and tie it around the head (of the goat), you treat it like a dead (person), you honour it. The patient rises and leaves through the door. The exorcist recites three times the (Sumerian) incantation: '. . .'. The patient takes(?) one of the (funerary) gifts with his garment (?) and gives it to the exorcist. While (the patient) leaves through the door the exorcist utters a cry and declares: 'He (i.e. the patient) has died!'; he performs a lamentation. You shall perform the funerary rites before Ereškigal three times(?), you place a soup still hot, you praise, you honour, you libate water, beer, milk, honey, butter (and) oil, you perform the funerary rites for the ghosts of the family, you perform funerary rites for the goat, before Ereškigal you recite the (Sumerian) incantation: 'The big brother is her brother', you treat the goat with respect, as if it were alive, and bury it, you offer barley for [the goat(?)], for Ereškigal and for the ghosts of his family.
(*LKA* no. 79, 1–29 and *KAR* No. 245, 1–22, see Tsukimoto, 1985: 125–8; rest of the ritual is broken off)

Substitutes could also be objects, for instance a reed effigy or clay figurine. According to a Sumerian incantation on a tablet from Babylon (Seleucid period), the measurements of the man were first taken and the reed substitute was therefore probably life-sized (*CT* 17 pl. 15 I 20–6, for a translation of the incantation see Thompson, 1904: 56–9). In other cases a clay figurine is used. It lies together with the patient during the night and next morning the figurine is brought out into the steppe and placed facing the rising sun. Black and white hairs from a goat are put on the figurine which may mean that it had the shape of a kid and not of a man (the texts, however, are not exact on this point; see the incantation *CT* 17 pl. 29–30, lines 30–40 and duplicate *CT* 17 pl. 30 Tablet 'S', cf. Thompson, 1904: 100–3; also *STT* II no. 173, 23–70). All these techniques are described in bilingual incantations, not in the instructions for the exorcist.

The Ritual for the Substitute King

Whether to choose a sheep or a figurine as a substitute might have depended on the affluence of the sick person. The seemingly most effective substitute, a human being, was reserved for the king on special occasions, namely when a lunar eclipse was considered a serious danger to the person of the sovereign. In prayers to various deities a plea is inserted for averting the evil from the king in such situations: 'From the evil predicted by the lunar eclipse which happened on the ..th day of the month NN, the evil of omens and portents foretelling evil and bad things which occurred in my palace and my land (please free me!)' (for this phrase see Mayer, 1976: 100–2). To escape this danger the king was dethroned and another person pro forma made king instead. After a certain period, one hundred days at maximum, the mock king was put to death and when the portended evil had thus come true, the real king could take over again. Such human sacrifices (in effect) had a long tradition in Mesopotamia. The oldest case, mentioned in a late chronicle, is that of a king of Isin in the nineteenth century BC. The irony of this event is that the real king died anyway and the substitute king remained on the throne:

> Erra-imitti, the king, installed Enlil-bani, the gardener as sub-stitute king on his throne. He placed the royal tiara on his head. Erra-imitti [died] in his palace when he sipped a hot broth. Enlil-bani, who occupied the throne, did not give it up (and) so was sovereign.
> (Grayson, 1975: 155)

About 1300 BC a similar ritual was in use in the Hittite kingdom and several Babylonian terms in the Hittite instructions for the ceremony show that Mesopotamia was the origin of this custom (see Kümmel, 1968).

Most sources for the substitute king date from the Neo-Assyrian period, especially the reign of Esarhaddon (680–669 BC) (see Parpola, 1983: XXII–XXXII with a catalogue of sources). From the astrologers' reports to the king we learn that lunar eclipses were extremely unfavourable to the king, yet not every eclipse required the enthronement of a substitute king. It depended on which part of the moon was eclipsed whether the king of Assyria, of Babylonia, or of another country was meant. A total eclipse afflicted all the kings of the world. However, if the planet Jupiter was visible during the eclipse the king would remain well and no substitute would be required. During sixteen reported eclipses between 680 and 666 BC a substitute king was enthroned in eight cases, but even if the eclipse did not concern the king directly, the performance of a high number of apotropaic rituals and lamentations was recommended.

During the reign of a substitute king the real king had to live in seclusion and not to show himself in public, but there is no doubt that he still acted as the ruler and made the decisions. The substitute king was allowed to enjoy life as much as possible; administrative texts show that he had a court of considerable size, a substitute queen is also mentioned, and a royal banquet was daily prepared for him. His staff included cooks and musicians as well as several bodyguards, certainly to prevent his escape. The person chosen as substitute was most probably a criminal condemned to death or a prisoner of war, although a loyal subject of the king could conceivably have given his own life willingly to save the king. The texts do not go into details on this point or on the question of how the substitute king and his queen were put to death, but in any case they were given a royal burial with all appropriate rites. The following quotations are both from letters referring to a total lunar eclipse in the year 671 BC:

The substitute king, who on the 14th sat on the throne in [Ninev]eh and spent the night of the 15th in the palace of the king, (and) on whom the eclipse took place, entered the city of Akkad (i.e. Babylon) safely on the night of the 20th (and) sat upon the throne. I made him recite the scribal recitations before the Sun god, he took all the celestial and terrestrial omens on himself, (and) ruled all the countries.
(Translation by Parpola, 1970: 227, no. 279)

'[Damqî], the son of the bishop (chief temple administrator) of Akka[de (i.e. Babylonia)], who had ruled Assyria, Babylonia and all the countries, [di]ed with his queen on the night o[f the ..th day as] a substitute for the king, my lord, [and for the sake of the li]fe of [the prince] Šamaš-šumu-ukin. He went to his destiny for their rescue.

We prepared the burial chamber. He and his queen have been decorated, treated, displayed, buried (and) wailed over. The burnt-offering has been burnt, all omens have been cancelled, (and) numerous apotropaic rituals, *bit rimki* (and) *bit salā' mê* ceremonies, exorcistic rites, *eršahunga* rites (and) scribal recitations have been performed in perfect manner. The king, my lord, should know this.

(Translation by Parpola, 1970: 229, no. 280)

The significance of the substitute king ritual is shown by the fact that a similar ceremony is mentioned by several classical authors (see the list in Parpola, 1983: XXIX–XXXI). Especially interesting is an episode described by the biographers of Alexander the Great. Shortly before his death in 323 BC Alexander came to Babylon, although the Chaldean diviners had warned him against entering the city because of evil portents that they had observed. Thereupon, a man appeared in the palace, clad as the king, and seated himself on the throne. When questioned he told how he had been a prisoner but had been freed from his chains and commanded to go to the palace and act like this. Alexander, regarding this as a bad omen, was frightened and on the advice of the diviners the man was killed (thus Plutarch, *Lives*, Alexander LXXIII–IV and, with some variations, Arrian, *Anabasis* VII 24 and Diodorus Siculus, *Library of Universal History* XVII 116, all quoted by Parpola, 1983: XXIX–XXX). Apparently the Greeks misunderstood this incident which in fact must have been a substitute king ritual, arranged by the diviners in order to dispel the evil that menaced the king after he had ignored their warnings (see Kümmel, 1968: 293).

Not only the king but the people as well had reason to fear an eclipse. From the Seleucid period parts of a ritual against the evil of a lunar eclipse are known. Lamentations are performed and as soon as the eclipse starts the priest sets fire to cedar, tamarisk and other woods on a brazier; the fire must not go out as long as the eclipse lasts. During the eclipse the people must cover their heads with their clothes and recite apotropaic conjurations. The next day the brazier and apotropaic drawings made with flour are removed and everything is thrown into the river. Purification rituals are performed in the temples, especially in the temple of the moon god Sin, and long Sumerian incantations must be recited, among them a story of the seven evil demons attacking the moon. These and other rites to be performed during the eclipse show that the evil was supposed to be defeated by light and by lamentations and shouting (BRM 4 no. 6, see Ebeling, 1931b: 92–6).

Ghosts

Ghosts are often mentioned as the cause of diseases in the diagnostic handbooks, and several medical texts are concerned with therapy against the symptoms of affliction by ghosts, called 'Hand of a ghost' or 'When a ghost has seized a man'. The medications are potions, salves, amulets in leather bags or fumigations. The reason for a ghost to appear was mostly assumed to be irregularities during funerary rites or the cessation of the offerings to the dead, for instance if there were no remaining relatives to care for the deceased family members. The ghost of someone who had died in an accident, of a criminal who might have been sentenced to death or of someone who had not been buried at all was especially likely to persecute the living. (For the belief in ghosts and medications and rituals against them, see Bottéro, 1984; for funerary rites and the care of the dead, Tsukimoto, 1985.) The various possibilities are often listed in incantations: 'The ghost which has set itself on me, persecutes me, [does not depart from me] day and [night], be it a strange ghost, a forgotten ghost, a ghost the name of which is not mentioned, a ghost which has no one to care for it (. . .), a ghost which was killed by a weapon, a ghost which died for a sin against a god or an offence against a king' (translation by Castellino, 1955: 245, lines 6–9); or in a similar context: 'Be it a ghost which has a (regular) burial, or a ghost that had it not, or a ghost that has no brother and sister, or a ghost which has nobody to mention its name, or a ghost of its family, a roving ghost, or a ghost that was abandoned in the steppe' (translation by Castellino, 1955: 249, lines 23–5). The persecuting ghost could also be that of a father or mother, or of other relatives, and sometimes a diagnosis identifies the kind of ghost responsible for the symptoms: 'If his stomach is afflicted (both) when he rises and when he sits: the ghost of a brother or a sister has seized him', or, with symptoms in the face and throat: 'The hand of a roving ghost has seized him in the desert' (Labat, 1951: 114–15, line 34', and 76–7, line 62).

The rituals against ghosts mainly aimed at relieving the neglect of the cult of the dead by pouring out water and flour to the ghost, by burying an image of it or by presenting the regular funerary offerings. A hoof or a horn of an ox was often used for pouring water: 'You (the exorcist) wash his (the patient's) hands with soap and powdered gypsum and say thus: 'Šamaš, the evil ghost which you know, but I do not know, may it not approach, come near, draw close, block its way!' You shall say thus and fill the hoof of an ox with water, pour *šeguššu* (late barley?) flour into it, before Šamaš stir it up with a rush, libate it and the ghost will disappear' (Castellino, 1955: 251, lines 33–5).

In the following ritual the figurine of the ghost is apparently not buried but burned in order to dispel the evil:

If a ghost seizes a man, stays in his body [. . .], if he is repeatedly panicked by the ghost [. . .]: Its ritual: In the afternoon you sweep the ground (and) sprinkle pure water; you set up a censer (with) juniper, you libate first-rate beer. You mix clay from the pit, tallow (and) wax and make a figurine of the ghost that causes panic, you put horn of an ox (on it) (and) give it the face of a man. You write its name on its left shoulder:

'This is the figurine of the ghost causing panic and evil disease of NN, son of NN!' Before Šamaš the patient shall lift this figurine with his left (hand) and . . . with his right. You shall let him say the incantation 'Šamaš, this is the figurine of (the ghost causing) panic' three times and place (the figurine) in a *burzigallu* (a large bowl). You lift the torch and recite the incantation 'Girru, you are fierce, you are furious!' three times. You undo the cultic arrangement, you prostrate yourself and throw the burnt material into the desert area and he will recover.

(*KAR* no. 267, 1–11 and *LKA* No. 85 rev. 22–31, see Ebeling, 1931b: 138)

The instructions for a similar ritual, written on the same tablet as the one just quoted, are rather broken, but the incantation, addressing Šamaš, Ea and Marduk, describes how the figurine of the ghost is treated. It is provided with clothes and food and sent to the west where the sun enters the nether world at sunset. This practice is also used to expel evil demons:

This is the image (of the ghost),
Šamaš, in your presence I have sought him out, I gave him
    clothes to clothe himself, shoes for his feet,
A girdle for his waist; a waterskin that he may drink water
    (and)
Travel provisions I have assigned (to him). May he go
    towards the sunset,
May he be entrusted to Nedu, the gatekeeper of the nether
    world!
(*KAR* no. 267 rev. 10–13, see Ebeling, 1931b: 141;
    Falkenstein and von Soden, 1953: 341)

Moreover, funerary offerings were often brought to the ghosts of the patient's family in order to obtain their help against the evil:

If a ghost seizes a man and stays in his body and does not [let go]: At sunset you let Šamaš know, you purify(?) the ghost of

his family and his kin. In the morning you set up a reed altar, you place twelve small loaves (on it) [. . .], you heap up dates and flour, you set up a censer (with) juniper, you place a [. . .] of silver. You place this before Šamaš. You bring funerary offerings to the ghost of his family, [you bring(?)] a present(?) [. . .]. You lift your hands and say as follows to Šamaš.
(The rest of the ritual is broken; *LKA* no. 84, 1–6, see Tsukimoto, 1985: 170–1)

Offerings were presented to deceased members of a family on certain occasions, especially the last day, the twenty-ninth, of the month Abu. This is also the date for performing a ritual to expel the ghosts of the father and mother (*BAM* IV no. 323, 79–88 and duplicate, see Farber, 1977: 211–13).

Evil Portents and Apotropaic Rituals

Collections of omens and portents are a literary genre in a large number of tablets. The series *Šumma alu* ('If a city') alone comprises at least 174 tablets; these so-called terrestrial omens indicate various signs to be observed in the city, in nature and in the behaviour of people and animals. Others, for instance in the series *Šumma izbu* ('If an anomaly'), deal with physical defects or peculiarities of newborn animals and babies, while others again are concerned with human physiognomy or celestial omens (see for example Leichty, 1970). All such signs, it was believed, could foretell something about the fate of the person involved, or portended evil, indicating that the gods were angry with that person, because he had committed a sin, or had for some reason become impure. The more significant the sign was, the more far-reaching were the consequences. Normally, the appearance of a lizard in a house, for instance, or a screaming cat would concern only the person who had observed it, but signs like earthquakes or lunar eclipses were a menace to the king and the whole land.

The Mesopotamians sought to avert the portended evil by a certain kind of ritual called *namburbi*, a Sumerian term meaning literally 'its undoing'. About 140 such rituals are known, most of them from the Assyrian libraries of the seventh century BC, but the genre is undoubtedly of Babylonian origin (for the *namburbi* rituals, see Caplice, 1974). There are *namburbi* rituals for special situations, like 'to remove the evil of partridges which gather over a man' or '*Namburbi* for the evil of a dog which howls (and) moans in a man's house, or spatters its urine upon a man' (Caplice, 1967: 276, line 20' and 1974: 17, line 10). Sometimes such apotropaic instructions were also written in the omen series as an addition to the omen in question, and there are also rituals of a general character to avert any possible evil portended by a sign. A large part of the *namburbi* texts have been found in Nineveh in the library of Assurbanipal and the performance of such rituals is frequently reported in the letters to the king, but as a rule the *namburbi* rituals can be classified as 'handbooks for performance of private apotropaic rites' (Caplice, 1974: 7). Normally the participants in a ritual were only two: the exorcist and the person who had observed the omen and was therefore directly concerned by it. Sometimes a purification of the house where the portent had been seen was required too. Since the portended evil was thought to point to a disharmony in the relations between man and gods due to some offence or impurity, the purpose of a *namburbi* was twofold. On the one hand, the object portending the evil had to be 'undone', either concretely by destroying it or getting rid of it (for instance a malformed animal was thrown into the river), or by an act of sympathetic magic (a clay image of a dog that howled was thrown into the river). On the other hand, the man had to be cleansed and freed from his sin. This was also performed both as a physical cleansing by washing with pure water or bathing in the river and as a merely symbolic action by stripping off the garment and putting on a clean one. The dispelling of the evil was, however, only possible through the intervention of the gods. They alone could free the man from its consequences. Therefore offerings (bread, cake, dates, beer and incense, and in some cases a sheep) were made and prayers were also part of the ritual. The gods invoked were most frequently Šamaš, god of justice, and Ea and Marduk as gods of magic. Moreover, as in other rituals, the fire or the river which assisted in destroying the evil were often addressed as well.

Every unusual event seems to have been feared as a bad omen and such cases were even reported to the king as for instance when a fox had entered the city of Aššur and fallen into a well in the temple garden. The fox was brought up and killed in order to dispel the evil portent, although it is not mentioned that a *namburbi* was performed (Parpola, 1970: 62–3, no. 92 obv. 6 – rev. 3). The large collections of omens were studied by the diviners when they searched for an interpretation of a current sign, and if an event could not be found in the written sources they tried to explain it in some way or other by analogies. The reports are often reassuring in trying not to alarm the king, as in this letter to Esarhaddon (seventh century BC):

> It has quaked: that is bad. They should perform the ritual against the earthquake, your gods will (then) make (the evil) pass by. 'Ea has done, Ea has undone'.[13] He who caused the earthquake has also created the apotropaic ritual against it. Was there no earthquake in the time of the king's fathers (and) grandfathers? Did I not see earthquakes when I was small? The god has (only) wanted to open the ears of the king: 'He should pray to the god, perform the apotropaic ritual (and) be on the alert.'
> (Translation by Parpola, 1970: 24–5, no. 35)

Most of the omen interpretations quoted by the Assyrian scholars, and those found in hemerologies and other divination compendia, sound like primitive peasants' weather maxims; for instance, 'When it thunders on a cloudless day: there will be darkness (or) there will be famine in the land' (Thompson, 1900 vol. II: lxxv, no. 235 rev. 7–8). In fact, from the sixth century BC onwards, Babylonian scholars systematically recorded information about the weather, prices, accidents and water levels of the Euphrates, together with astronomical observations, in order to improve their knowledge about the relationship of celestial phenomena and such events. In other words, they did not totally rely on tradition but sought to establish an empirical basis for divination by collecting as much data as possible.

Divination

Even the earliest textual sources from Mesopotamia give examples of divination. In the third millennium, for instance, certain priests were nominated by extispicy, i.e. the examination of the entrails of a sacrificial animal, mostly a sheep. Other methods were the observation of oil drops in water or of the shapes of smoke from a censer, and there are also instances of decisions concerning important questions being sought in dreams. These latter techniques were simple and inexpensive and probably widely used, but instructions concerning performance and interpretation became only exceptionally a part of the scholarly literature of the first millennium BC. Conversely, extispicy remained the preferred divination method in royal and state affairs (for divination and an outline of various methods, see Reiner, 1960a; Sumerian sources: Falkenstein, 1966; dreams: Oppenheim, 1956; oil omens: Pettinato, 1966; extispicy: Jeyes, 1989; Starr, 1983). Most popular of all was astrology, and during the first millennium BC it seems to have overshadowed other kinds of divination, and stars were even conjured in magic rituals. Stars were also frequently addressed when asking for a sign in a particular matter, for instance to be seen in a dream or by the flight of birds, and they were also invoked when evil portents were to be averted. The reason for addressing stars in these situations was probably that they were considered to produce the most reliable signs and predictions for the future. There are thus examples of the stars being asked to confirm an omen obtained by extispicy or in a dream.

An outstanding text from the seventh century BC describes several divination techniques; for instance, a prayer to the gods of the night is to be recited three times over a tamarisk branch and a sign drawn at the head of the bed. After this the person should go to bed and will then see a sign (*STT* I no. 73, 44–51, see Reiner, 1960a). Further, on the same tablet there are instructions for sprinkling an ox with water and observing its reactions in order to get a sign. Although this divination method seemingly has nothing to do with astronomical phenomena in the broadest sense, it is performed 'before the gods of the night' and accompanied by a prayer to 'the gods, the judges in heaven', probably Šamaš and Adad, the sun and the weather god. The exorcist (who is most probably the executor of this ritual) then says: 'Let me see your true judgment and your divine decision, so that I may make a pronouncement. Let the ox provide a sign whether NN, son of NN, will have success' (Reiner, 1960a: 28). It seems that such rituals were carried out by the exorcist for a sick person, in order to find out whether he would recover or not. At any rate, a detailed description of the future was not sought by this method, but rather a simple Yes or No answer to an immediately approaching event, for instance whether to start a journey or not, or whether one would have success or not. Only one other text with similar instructions has been found, but such divination practices might have been more commonly used than these two instances suggest, at least in older periods. From the first millennium BC extispicy and astrology were predominant.

Necromancy

Evidence of necromancy is scarce in the magical literature, but there is no doubt that it was practised, probably already at the beginning of the second millennium BC. The most prominent example is that of the Gilgameš Epic where Enkidu's ghost is allowed to escape for a short time to answer Gilgameš' questions about the conditions in the land of the dead. During the second and first millennium BC there are scattered references to the practice of necromancy but generally these are without details and difficult to interpret. Not until the Neo-Assyrian, Neo- and Late Babylonian periods are there real instructions for performing necromancy. (Sources for necromancy were collected by Finkel, 1983–4; to these add von Weiher, 1983: 100–3, no. 20; and *BAM* III no. 215, 44–63; for necromancy rituals, see also Tropper, 1989: 83–109, 118–25.)

The rituals make use of a human skull or figurines representing either a ghost of a deceased person or the deity and evil demon, Namtar, bringer of death, whose name literally means '[divine] decree'. In addition, a salve of oil, herbs and other ingredients is produced. In some cases the figurine or the skull is anointed, in others the eyes or face of the man who wants to question the ghost: 'You recite the incantation three times and you anoint your eyes, and you will see the ghost: he will speak with you. You can look at the ghost: he will talk with you' (translation by Finkel, 1983–4: 10). According to one of the incantations the ghost was assumed to appear inside the skull: 'May he bring up a ghost from the darkness for me! May he [put life back(?)] into the dead man's limbs! I call upon you, O skull of skulls: May he who is within the skull answer [me!] O Šamaš, who brings light in (lit. who opens) the darkness' (translation by Finkel, 1983–4: 9, ii 3'–6'). The beginning is broken so it is not clear who is to bring the ghost – perhaps Šamaš who in the night went through the Nether world? In another prescription, preserved in both a Neo-Assyrian copy and on a tablet from Seleucid Uruk, the first divine pair, Enmešarra and Ninmešarra, father and mother of all gods, are invoked in an incantation to be recited over a mixture of water, oil and a plant called *anameru*, occasionally used in medicine: 'On the twenty-ninth of the month Abu you anoint your face (with it) and the Anunnaki will talk with you' (*BAM* III no. 215 rev. 44–63, see Köcher, 1966: 18; and von Weiher, 1983: 101–2, lines 9–27). Anunnaki, originally a collective name for the gods of the Sumerian pantheon, are in later periods gods of the Nether world, horrifying and ominous since they decide the fate of human beings. The people of ancient Mesopotamia honoured the Anunnaki and brought them regular offerings, usually on the last day of the month, in the hope that they would grant long life and keep the evil ghosts and demons in the Nether world (see Tsukimoto, 1985: 184–200).

The instructions for necromancy are in all instances quite brief and it is therefore uncertain how the manifestation of the ghost was expected – whether while the person was awake or in a dream, as in the other occasions of fortune-telling. Judging from several rituals averting evil from ghosts it was not uncommon to see, hear or dream of deceased family members or foreigners and it usually caused terror, since it portended evil and death.

Astrology

The main reason for astronomical observations in ancient Babylonia was the belief that celestial phenomena could foretell what would happen in the future. Although no astronomical observations are attested from the third millennium BC the importance of the heavenly bodies is evident from other sources, for instance in connection with the calendar. Further, the movements of the stars were probably paraphrased in poetic terms in Sumerian myths, and there is evidence that important questions like building a temple were decided by astronomical omens. Some of the most important and oldest deities of ancient Mesopotamia were celestial: the sun god (Utu/*Šamaš*), the moon god (Nanna/*Sîn*) and the Venus star (Inanna/*Ištar*). The highest god was originally Heaven (An/*Anu*), later displaced by Enlil, the god of the air and the storm.

As time passed, astrology gained more and more significance and subtle methods to interpret these portents were developed. Records of systematic observations of the planet Venus go back to the Old Babylonian period but most of the astronomical texts are from the first millennium BC, for instance a large compendium of omens called from the initial line *Enuma Anu Enlil*, 'When Anu and Enlil', and containing about 7,000 omens written on a total of 70 tablets. The astronomical omens concern exclusively the country and the king, never the fate of an individual. Horoscopes in our modern sense were not developed until the last centuries BC but the principles, the forerunner of the zodiac, and the belief in the influence of the stars were already present in Babylonian astrology. (For *Enuma Anu Enlil*, see Rochberg-Halton, 1988; for Babylonian astronomy and astrology in general, see van der Waerden, 1980.)

At the Neo–Assyrian court, astronomers reported regularly to the king about celestial phenomena and their importance for the future and for the decisions of the king. If evil was portended the scholars would suggest the performance of a ritual, as in the following letter from a 'scribe' (i.e. astronomer) to the king. This quotation also demonstrate how the ancient scholars distinguished between (a) the canonical written tradition called 'Series' in which the omens were rendered in a fixed order, (b) 'other literary sources' not included in the Series, and (c) oral tradition. The first of these was certainly considered the most reliable:

> When the planet Mars comes out from the constellation Scorpio, turns (and) re-enters Scorpio, its interpretation is this:
>
> If Mars, having returned, enters Scorpio, do not neglect your guard; the king should not go outdoors on an evil day. This omen is not from the Series (but) is from the oral tradition of the masters.
>
> When Mars, furthermore, turns from the head of the constellation Leo and afflicts Cancer (and) Gemini, its interpretation is this: End of the reign of the king of the Westland. This is not from the Series (but) is non-canonical.
>
> This aforesaid is the only area which is held for bad, if Mars turns there. Wherever else it might turn, it may happily do so, there is no word about it.
>
> (Translation by Parpola, 1970: 8–11, no. 13 obv. 21-rev. 12)

Prayers to stars are comparatively rare in magic rituals. The initial incantation of the anti-witchcraft ritual Maqlû, 'I call you, gods of the night!', is addressed to the stars, since it is performed during the night. *Zikurudû* too was carried out before stars, Ursa Major or Scorpio, and the counteractions were made facing these same stars. Other rituals addressing stars are generally related to the night or to divination, but not necessarily to astrology. For instance, a ritual against insomnia contains a long prayer to the gods of the night. The constellation Ursa Major seems to have been the most popular group of stars invoked in magic rituals, but altogether the examples are few and random. Other stars mentioned several times in incantations are the Pleiades, for instance in this love charm: a female figurine is made of tallow and an incantation addressing the Pleiades and Mercury is recited over it, but beer is libated before Ištar (*KAR* no. 69, 6–19, see Biggs, 1967: 74). The stars, moreover, were believed to influence medications in a favourable way. In the medical prescriptions the drugs are often to be prepared in the evening and placed 'under the stars' until next morning. Water, used for purifications, was also mixed with certain herbs at sunset and treated in the same way. Sometimes it is explicitly mentioned that the medication should face the Goat star, i.e. the constellation Lyra, the star of Gula, goddess of healing. (For stars and magic see Reiner, 1985.)

Prayers and rituals were to be performed on favourable days, as listed in the hemerologies, but this principle could be applied more subtly; a certain ritual was not expected to be equally successful on any day of a year. Calendars were developed according to the pattern: if in month NN on day X the ritual so-and-so is performed, it will succeed. The reasons for combining rituals with certain dates are obscure; it may be an old tradition although such lists are not known before the Neo-Assyrian period:

> If in the month Abu on the tenth day (the ritual against) *zikurudû* sorcery is performed, (or), on the tenth day (the ritual against) IGI.NIGIN.NA (an eye disease)), (or) on the twenty-eighth day (the ritual against the diseases) *antašubbû, bennu* (and) Lugal-urra and the Hand of the God or to seize away the hand of a ghost – it will succeed.
> (*STT* II no. 300, 14–15)

This text is organized chronologically from the first month, Nisan, through the year, to the twelfth month. It does not mention every day of the month, but usually only the first, the tenth, the twenty-first or the twenty-eighth. Later, in the Seleucid period, when the astrological element of magic was getting more important, such information was combined with stars and signs of the zodiac: '*zikurudû*: the star Sagittarius; (or) secondly: the star Gemini. IGI.NIGIN.NA: The star Gemini' (BRM 4 no. 20 obv. 9–10, for this text, see Ungnad, 1941–4).

MESOPOTAMIAN MAGIC AFTER THE FALL OF BABYLON

In the earliest periods magic texts together with other literary works had already spread outside the borders of Mesopotamia; Sumerian incantations from the third millennium BC, for instance, have been found in Ebla in the West (for these texts, see Krebernik, 1984). But the influence was also felt in the other direction: incantations in Elamite, and probably also Hurrian, are attested in Babylonia from the Old Babylonian period and the demon Lamaštu was possibly of Elamite origin (see van Dijk, 1987). Trade routes and military campaigns moved far away from Mesopotamia both towards the East and the West and with the distribution of cuneiform writing and Babylonian as a lingua franca in the middle of the second millennium, Babylonian literature and religious ideas certainly became known in wide parts of the ancient Near East. In Ugarit, near the coast of the Mediterranean Sea, Babylonian literary and scholarly works dating from the fifteenth century BC have been found and some of these were even translated into Ugaritic. The archives of the Hittite capital Hattuša (fourteenth century BC) contained several texts in Babylonian, and others concerning magic and divination, and Hittite as well as bilingual versions of various genres, are attested, for instance extispicy, hemerologies, astrological and other omen types. The Hittites were certainly influenced by the Babylonians in the field of magic but they also had a tradition of their own which differed considerably from the Mesopotamian one. Nevertheless, Babylonian ways of thinking might have found their way to the Mediterranean world through the Hittite culture. Thus it has been suggested that the Etruscans' knowledge of and interest in birth omens might have stemmed from the Hittite-Babylonian tradition, since such omen collections in Babylonian, Hittite and Hurrian were found in Hattuša (Leichty, 1970: 20). In the first millennium BC it was probably Aramaic-speaking people who were the important carriers of ideas over great parts of the Near

East (see Oppenheim, 1964: 309), playing a role similar to that played by the Greeks in the Hellenistic period.

The Mesopotamian intellectual achievement which was most respected in Antiquity was astrology. It was often stated that the Babylonians were the first to make astronomical observations and to have done this over a considerable period of time. In classical Antiquity astrology was often attributed especially to the Chaldeans, originally the name of a western Semitic nomadic tribe, in the first millennium living in the southern Babylonian cities. The last independent Babylonian kings, among them Nebuchadnezzar, were Chaldeans. Both classical authors and the Old Testament repeatedly allude to Babylonian (or Assyrian) diviners, soothsayers and magicians, and with justice; the Babylonians did have a long tradition of making astronomical observations, divination and magic did play an important role in everyday life, and magicians and diviners were indeed prominent advisers of the king. But the ancient authors also succumbed to prejudices and were ignorant of the real state of things, as demonstrated by the Greek authors' descriptions of the substitute king ritual referred to above.

Thus, the cultural exchange between Mesopotamia and its neighbours took place over a long period and it is difficult to track the fortunes of elements like magic practices and magic belief, whereas written sources such as incantations or prescriptions for the performance of rituals can be located more successfully in various periods and in different locations. The Babylonian magic literature, reaching back into the third millennium BC, does not seem to have outlasted cuneiform writing. As this was given up in the last centuries BC, most of the literature handed down in this medium was forgotten. The only exception, apparently, was astronomical texts, whereas the scholarly tradition in the field of magic sank into oblivion. Magic texts seem not to have been translated into Aramaic, Persian or Greek. This is undoubtedly due to their esoteric character and position as secret knowledge, which meant that they probably did not reach out beyond the small circle of scholars and magicians at the temples in Babylon, Uruk and other cities in the late period.

Whereas the Greeks were highly interested in Babylonian astrology and divination they cared less about the history, religion or mythology of the ancient civilization, as is shown in the case of the work *Babyloniaka* written in Greek by Berossos, a Babylonian and contemporary of Alexander the Great. This account of Babylonian history and culture was little read in Antiquity with the exception of the parts concerning astronomy, and the work itself is entirely lost, only a small number of quotations from an abridgement from the first century being known today (for Berossos's work, see Burstein, 1978). Babylonian myths and also some parts of the scholarly works were, in the eyes of the Greeks, too barbarian or obsolete to be worth dealing with. The few pieces of cuneiform literature written with Greek letters found in Babylonia and dating from the last centuries BC are therefore certainly not an attempt to present these texts to Greek readers but served rather as an aid for Graeco-Babylonian scribes who were no longer acquainted with the Babylonian language.

Although the Babylonian magical and medico-magical traditions have much in common with magic in classical Antiquity as regards certain practices and principles, there are also considerable differences. In the works of classical authors accounts of necromancy, love charms, manipulation with demonic powers and other occult and supernatural phenomena are predominant. The Babylonian magical texts, however, are instead prescriptions for communication with the divine. Their purpose is to purify a person in a real and figurative sense, to free him from sins and everything which may disturb his relations to the gods. They are also concerned with finding out the will of the gods in order to act properly and obtain divine goodwill and protection. The magical rituals are therefore expressions of religious behaviour in everyday situations as well as in cases of illness or distress and should be understood as a means for maintaining the harmony between man and the divine. The exorcist did not have authority to command the demons directly, nor did he possess any super-natural powers; he merely appealed to the gods for help and acted at their command. A major part of the magical practices was thus closely connected with Babylonian religion, and it is certainly not a coincidence that these texts were usually kept in temple libraries. Furthermore, the religious aspect of these rituals would probably have prevented their acceptance by foreigners. Texts with a more practical purpose, like the various handbooks of exorcists, diviners and physicians, were possibly not affected by such religious discrimination and so omen collections, lists of stones and plants with descriptions of their qualities, and similar works could well have attracted a broader interest, provided the scholars did not keep them secret, as might have been the case. But most of the scholarly magic tradition was bound to be forgotten and what remained was only a few names of gods and demons and, not least, a somewhat distorted picture of Babylo-nian magicians and diviners and their knowledge (see Thomsen, 1988). But even if the written tradition disappeared it is possible that magical practices of Babylonian origin survived in various contexts, for instance in Greek magical papyri (see Reiner, 1990: 422–3), or in Mandaic incantation bowls (see for instance Yamauchi, 1967: 62–3). Future studies will therefore probably reveal more affinities between Babylonian and European magic.

ABBREVIATIONS FOR PUBLICATIONS OF CUNEIFORM TEXTS

ABL   Robert Francis Harper, *Assyrian and Babylonian Letters Belonging to the Kouyunjik Collection of the British Museum*, vols 1–14, London, Chicago, 1892–1914.

ABRT   James Alexander Craig, *Assyrian and Babylonian Religious Texts*, vol. I, Leipzig, 1895; vol. II, Leipzig, 1897.

AMT   Reginald Campbell Thompson, *Assyrian Medical Texts*, London, 1923.

BAM   Franz Köcher, *Die babylonisch-assyrische Medizin in Tex-*

ten und Untersuchungen. Band I: Keilschrifttexte aus Assur, Berlin, 1963. Band II: Keilschrifttexte aus Assur 2, Berlin, 1963. Band III: Keilschrifttexte aus Assur 3, Berlin, 1964. Band IV: Keilschrifttexte aus Assur 4, Babylon, Nippur, Sippar, Uruk und unbekannter Herkunft, Berlin, 1971. Band V: Keilschrifttexte aus Ninive 1. Berlin, New York, 1980.

BMS   Leonard William King, *Babylonian Magic and Sorcery, Being 'The Prayers of the Lifting of the Hand'*. London, 1896.

BRM 4   Albert Tobias Clay, *Epics, Hymns, Omens, and Other Texts*. New Haven, 1923 (Babylonian Records in the Library of J. Pierpont Morgan, 4).

CT 17   Reginald Campbell Thompson, *Cuneiform Texts from Babylonian Tablets in the British Museum*, vol. 17, London, 1903.

CT 20   Reginald Campbell Thompson, *Cuneiform Texts from Babylonian Tablets in the British Museum*, vol. 20, London, 1904.

K   Tablets in the Kouyunjik collection of the British Museum.

KAR   Erich Ebeling, *Keilschrifttexte aus Assur religiösen Inhalts*. Leipzig, 1915–23.

LKA   Erich Ebeling, *Literarische Texte aus Assur*. Berlin, 1953.

PBS 1/2 Henry Frederick Lutz, *Selected Sumerian and Babylonian Texts*. Philadelphia, 1919 (University of Pennsylvania, the Museum, Publications of the Babylonian Section, 1/2).

STT I   Oliver R. Gurney and Jacob J. Finkelstein, *The Sultantepe Tablets*, I. London, 1957.

STT II   Oliver R. Gurney and Peter Hulin, *The Sultantepe Tablets*, II, London, 1964.

PART 2

Magic in Ancient Syria–Palestine – and in the Old Testament

Frederick H. Cryer

The Social-Historical Problem

Anyone who attempts to write on social phenomena in a vanished age is immediately confronted by two obvious problems, and a third, namely: why are we interested in the problem in question? lurks in the background of all such undertakings. Let us take the last, first: why are we concerned with the topic of magic in ancient Israel and Judah (Syria–Palestine, as I prefer simply to use the geohistorical rather than the political designations)? In other words, why are we concerned with the region of the southern Levant, rather than, say, with ancient Anatolia, Mesopotamia or Egypt, as all the civilizations in these regions have left massive literary deposits bearing on the phenomenon of magic, whereas our region has left virtually only the Old Testament, plus a handful of texts from ancient Ugarit and Qumran? It should also go without saying that the Old Testament is not a history, even though this observation conflicts with the understanding of earlier great Old Testament scholars such as the German, Gerhard von Rad, who once, famously, declared that 'The Old Testament is a history-book' (for recent studies that seriously challenge the notion of 'history' in connexion with the Old Testament, see Lemche, 1985 and 1988; Davies, 1995 and Thompson, 1992 and 1999). Nor is the Old Testament in its present form a document which is contemporary with the events it relates, even though it no doubt contains some valid information about much earlier times. The burden of this remark is merely to point out that the Old Testament cannot be regarded as what a historian would term a 'primary source' for studying the events it relates.

Here it would be best to be entirely candid: the Syrian-Palestinian region attracts the attention of ancient historians and social historians because it was, within a very narrow segment of the 100,000-odd years that Syria–Palestine has been inhabited by men, the birthplace of two of the great religions, Judaism and Christianity, which have left an abiding impression on the West, and which were themselves of decisive importance for the evolution of a third great religious tradition, that of Islam, which is also very much active today. Moreover, a great deal of theological research and history of religions in the nineteenth century and later has assured us that the inhabitants of ancient Syria–Palestine differed decisively with respect to so-called 'primitive' social and cultural features – including, of course, magic – found elsewhere in the ancient world. Thus it has long been claimed that, among other things, the inhabitants of the ancient states of Israel and Judah were prohibited from practising magic (cf., e.g., Blau, 1898)

In other words, we are interested in the region in question because of cultural influences present in *our* world today. Furthermore, the Islamic sector of our world is not much concerned with this question; only the regions of Jewish and Christian cultural influence are. Hence it can be argued that any such undertaking is implicitly Europo-centric, or, better, occidento-centric, reflecting almost entirely the religio-cultural concerns of Europe and the regions where European culture has exercised determinative influence.

Additionally, the point of departure for the investigation has already been established by pre-existing assumptions about the behaviour and nature of the people(s) who lived in the region in antiquity. I would not go so far as to claim that our preoccupation with our own tradition destroys the object of study; but it would be appropriate to consider the distortion automatically caused by the interests that govern our investigations. In this connexion, special emphasis has been called by the British scholar, Keith W. Whitelam (Whitelam, 1996), to the fact that such a one-sided stress on these very few centuries in the whole historical panorama of the region relegates all the other centuries, and the peoples and events who characterized them, to insignificance. It denies them both a history and a venue. In this, Whitelam is surely right, but curiosity nevertheless persists as to the short period in question among both scholars and the wider public, and this justifies – at least to some extent – our concern with it.

But why *magic*? Again, we must be candid: a historian is concerned with an issue to the extent that that issue is perceived as germane to his or her own time, and the questions he or she is capable of devising to solve or illuminate the conundra under consideration are those made possible and relevant by the intellectual and social climate of his or her day. This is another way of saying that, as the very existence of this series of volumes indicates, our times have witnessed a renewed preoccupation with the 'occult', broadly defined as the whole range of extra-normal phenomena running from spiritism and the theosophical and spiritualist movements over Bigfoot and the Loch Ness monster to UFOs, pyramidology, some of the phenomena associated with New Age religion, satanism, crystallography and magic in general, including such 'magical' religions as voodoo and Santeria. And of course the burgeoning interest in these phenomena has been accompanied by the increasing relativization of Christianity and Judaism among the world's religions, as Westerners have shown increasing interest in Eastern and other religions since the first half of the nineteenth century. Thus 'magic', in one form or another – and I should hasten to emphasize the fact that the role played in contemporary Western societies by 'magical' phenomena today is hardly that which was played by 'magic' in the ancient 'high-cultural' societies, or even the more provincial ones of Syria–Palestine (see Cryer, 1994b: 41–95) – is a *contemporary* phenomenon in Western civilisation which stimulates the social historian's curiosity. And this contemporary interest will clearly also to some extent distort the view we can obtain of the past phenomena.

The two obvious problems I spoke of at the outset are those of *historical research* and *social anthropology*. In order to obtain relevant information for study, it is necessary to treat one's sources appropriately, as there is no source which simply vouches for its own authenticity, dates itself, establishes its relevance to a given question, or interprets itself appropriately. However, there is seldom agreement among historians of ancient or more recent times as to the precise means to these ends. As we shall see shortly, this problem is particularly acute in conjunction with the ancient history of Syria–Palestine. Moreover, it should be clear – and this is the second problem – that there is no consensus as to which method of sociological analysis best establishes the meaning and role of a given phenomenon in a given society.

Constructing Syrian-Palestinian History

I prefer the term 'constructing' in this connexion to the more usual 'reconstructing' in order to make the point that the concept of history designates either the raw facticity of one-damned-thing-after-another, that is, the unfolding of social life as lived, or the intellectual activity of using various kinds of evidence to produce a model of a given past. The latter is willy-nilly a creative activity involving the imagination and perceptiveness of the historian, acting, of course, within rigorous methodological constraints.

In conjunction with ancient Syrian-Palestinian society the situation in the historical research of the region has until recently consisted in large measure of the rationalizing re-telling of the Biblical narratives (this point is one of the main elements in the criticisms advanced by the so-called 'Copenhagen School' on traditional scholarly approaches to the early history of Israel and Judah; see already Lemche, 1985 and 1991; Cryer, 1994b; Thompson, 1992). These rationalized narratives have then been tricked out with the odd citation of the very few extra-Biblical written sources pertaining to Syria–Palestine, and with as much of the archaeological record as can be claimed to 'support' or 'cohere with' the Biblical narratives. Thus, for example, a nine-teenth-century commentary on the exodus narrative notes that the Israelites do not actually *see* Yahweh in the revelation on Sinai. Rather, he is enshrouded in fire and smoke. Hence, or so the author assumed, Mount Sinai was in reality a volcano and therefore was to be sought far to the south, seen from the Sinai desert. Such procedures likewise arrive at the conclusion that the history of 'ancient Israel' consisted of a putative 'patriarchal age', a sojourn in Egypt, an era of exodus and wandering in the desert, one of conquest and settlement, a period of government by a succession of judges, a monarchical period, an exile and a post-exilic period leading up to the rebuilding of the temple in Jerusalem and the restoration of the cult of Yahweh by his returned followers. This is a purely 'internal' understanding of the history of ancient Israel (it has formed the basis for such classical introductions to the history of Israel and Judah as Wellhausen, 1921; Noth, 1950; Donner, 1986 and others), and it is found nowhere outside the pages of the Old Testament, or in conservative works of 'Israelite' history which follow this approach (see above all Davies, 1995).

A prominent feature of the rationalizing and retelling approach is that it discards the Biblical chronology, according to which the creation of the world took place around 4004 BC (if we follow Ussher's reckoning; others, including the traditional rabbinical chronology, are also plausible candidates). The Old Testament chronology is, strictly speaking, an *anno mundi* chronology which takes its point of departure in the year of the creation, and dates everything else subsequent to that. However, the Biblical *anno mundi* chronology is badly out of synchronization with world history, to the extent that it intersects with the four to five thousand million years of history which the natural sciences point to with a great measure of agreement. It is likewise out of synch – although not by such vast margins!— with the astronomically based chronological systems of human history that were devised in Mesopotamia and Egypt, and hence ultimately with those of Greece and Rome, on which our own chronographic reckoning system for measuring historical time is ultimately based (see Cryer, 1987).

Hence, instead, adherents of the hybrid approach replace the Biblical *anno mundi* chronology on an ad hoc basis by one in which the 'patriarchs' are dated to about 1900–1600 BC, the sojourn in Egypt to *c.* 1600–1250 BC, the exodus to around 1250, the wilderness wandering and conquest of the land to around 1200, the period of the judges to *c.* 1200–1000, the period of monarchical rule from *c.* 1000 – 721 (in the northern kingdom) – 587 (in Judah), and the rebuilding of the temple to around 420. These various chronological periods have usually been supplied as needed by both archaeological and extra-Biblical (frequently textual) sources. But it is seldom considered that scholars advocating this approach simply discard the sections of the Old Testament chronology that conflict with modern natural-scientific knowledge without giving a thought to the fact that the lacunae and inaccuracies of the Israelite and Judaean chronology preserved in the books of Kings and elsewhere are equally problematical. They merely happen to be smaller. Logically, if one discards the former, then the latter, too, must be discarded. However, rationalization as it has been practised is a questionable business of intuitively rejecting some figures that strike a given scholar as non-'historical' while retaining others that strike him or her as plausible. It is worth mentioning in this context that *plausibility* is not a *historical* category, but a criterion for evaluating the verisimilitude of fictional literature. After all, was it at all *likely* that Napoleon would choose to remain in his tent at Waterloo, leaving the conduct of the battle to Marshal Ney?

In reality, none of the sources has been utilized on its own terms, but only in terms of some *other* source: the texts are 'illustrated' with archaeological materials, and the materials derive their interpretive framework from the literary record: a vicious circle of impressive dimensions. And in reality most Old Testament scholars writing in earlier times have regarded the Old Testament as a *privileged* source (it might be added that some still do), so that conflicts between statements in or implied by the Old Testament and either archaeological or extra-Biblical textual information have most often been resolved in favour of the Old Testament.

However, to a historian there are no privileged sources, a point that has gradually won adherents in Old Testament studies in recent years. The above-described picture has changed dramatically in Old Testament research during the last two decades. No evidence points to the centuries-long inhabitation of Egypt by sizeable groups of west semites during the second millennium BC. Hence the 400-year-long sojourn of the Israelites seems to fall by the board. Also, the overall archaeological picture has failed to substantiate, and in fact argues against the notion of an extensive settlement of foreigners in Syria–Palestine during the crucial transitional period between the Bronze and Iron ages (c. the thirteenth-eleventh centuries) (cf. Lemche, 1988, 109–17). It was in this period in which earlier Old Testament study placed the exodus of the enslaved Israelites from Egypt. However, it has become clear that the culture that existed at that time in Syria–Palestine carried on into the Iron Age and was essentially the same as that which had preceded it, if materially poorer; hence it cannot be claimed that the Biblical stories of the conquest and settlement of the land have a historical basis that is reflected in the archaeological record. Since there was an entity in Palestine called 'Israel' already in the thirteenth century (according to a reference in a stela by Pharaoh Merenptah), that quantity must have been a domestic social group (probably a tribe of some sort). Hence theories which see the evolution of the Israelite and Judaean societies out of the local populace have gained increasing ground among contemporary Old Testament scholars.

The obvious corollary to the insight that 'Israel' arose on the soil of Palestine is that the fundamental Biblical opposition between 'Israelites' and 'Canaanites' is also to be understood as an ahistorical construction, as has in particular been argued by the Danish scholar, N. P. Lemche (Lemche, 1991; and see now Garbini, 1997). It is important to emphasize this point, and to grasp its full implications, as the antithesis in question is fundamental to the Old Testament depiction of the establishment of the 'Israelites' in the land of promise; furthermore, the succumbing of the 'Israelites' to the allure of 'Canaanite' religion is assigned great importance in the books of Kings as the reason for Yahweh's abandoning his people to destruction. Hence dropping the antithesis between 'Israelite' and 'Canaanite' means discarding much of the history – particularly the religious history – of Israel and Judah as sketched out in the Old Testament.

Moreover, recent archaeological study in Israel has pointed towards the need to redate the pottery remains from the crucial tenth century (i.e. the putative 'era of David and Solomon') to about a century later (Finkelstein, 1996). This has removed a number of sites from consideration as major tenth-century urban centres; and this has in turn cast serious doubt on the actual historical background of the Biblical accounts of the empire of David and his son Solomon. This observation with respect to the pottery has lately seemed to find additional support in the fact that the gate complex at recently excavated Jezreel appears to have been of the multi-chambered, so-called 'Solomonic' sort (see Ussishkin and Woodhead, 1997), while the site itself is unquestionably from the ninth century. Hence, the other 'Solomonic' gates, by definition supposedly deriving from the tenth century, and in particular a much-discussed one in Megiddo, may also be dated to the ninth century, so that the entire connection with Solomon disappears.

Finally, other recent studies have indicated that the two states of Israel and Judah first achieved sufficient social integration to become urban societies, hence making possible the formation of territorial states, in the ninth and eighth centuries, respectively (Jamieson-Drake, 1991; Niemann, 1993). It is therefore unlikely that there ever was a unified 'Israel' that played a major role in the international politics of the close of the Bronze Age and the beginning of the Iron Age, which is what the Old Testament implies was the case. There was instead a small state of the same name whose fortunes we can follow at considerable distance from the first half of the ninth to the close of the eighth century. And this state had a companion state, Judah, which was possibly a client-state of the older and much larger state of Israel. We can trace Judah's fortunes from the end of the eighth to the end of the sixth century (and pick up the thread again much later, of course).

Given the disparity between the 'Israel' (and Judah) that we can reconstruct on the basis of the Old Testament literature and the picture of the two states that emerges from the study of the non-Biblical materials, a number of observations present themselves. The first is that the picture of 'Israel' in the Old Testament is an idealization that bears so little resemblance to what we otherwise know that its understanding is not served by attempting to compare it with a historical construction based on archaeological and extra-Biblical materials. It must instead be understood internally, on its own terms, as an 'Israel' of literature and not of historical fact, as has been trenchantly argued in recent times by the Welsh scholar Philip R. Davies (Davies, 1995). Furthermore, the *institutions* of this 'Biblical Israel' exist in the Old Testament, but it may not be assumed a priori that they existed in historical reality.

For our purposes, these observations imply that we shall be forced to offer a conjectural restoration of the histories of the two Syrian-Palestinian states of Israel and Judah as a background for an understanding of their respective societies.

Such a conjectural picture of this history is more easily produced than one might expect. All indications are that the territorial states of Israel and Judah existed, with monarchical governments based on dynastic succession, in the former case, between the early ninth and late eighth centuries, and, in the latter, between the early eighth and the early sixth centuries. After domination by the Neo-Assyrian and Neo-Babylonian empires, both territories were reconstituted towards the end of the sixth century as provinces of the Persian and, later (late fourth century), Macedonian-Greek, Syrian- and Egyptian-Greek imperial structures.

Material History
From the sixth to the first half of the fourth century, both regions were materially poorly off; the lack of centralized political administration meant a lack of that social stability which is essential for both trade and the long-term exploitation of the soil. Greek and

Hasmonaean struggles for hegemony over the region meant intermittent periods of social and political turmoil which ended in a period of self-rule, again based on hereditary monarchy (the Hasmonaeans). The third century and later saw considerable demographic growth, a trend that continued under the Romans until the first uprising against Roman domination. Altercations with the Roman overlord in the second half of the first century AD and again around the first third of the second century AD left the country of Judah/Judaea and the capital city of Jerusalem in ruins and the balance of the populace dispersed abroad. This situation changed dramatically almost two millennia later with the establishment of the modern state of Israel in AD 1948.

The economic life of the Israelite and Judaean societies (cf. Coote and Whitelam, 1987; Hopkins, 1985; Flanagan, 1988) was based on small farming, which included a variety of strategies for spreading the risks involved in agriculture in marginal regions so as to enable survival and economic viability. This means, in practice, that the small farmers not only had crops of cereals, but also bred small cattle such as sheep and goats. Small-cattle nomadism (cf. above all Lemche, 1985) enabled the exploitation of ecological niches in peripheral regions. Large holdings included olive trees and the practice of viniculture, but, all in all, the Syrian-Palestinian farmer's existence was marginal, and the econ-omies of the societies as a whole were subsistence economies. There were few raw materials and little surplus from farming or other sources so as to enable intensive specialization in handicrafts or artisanship, the production of goods for status and luxury purposes, the erection of monumental architectural structures, or the like, as was the case in Phoenicia. There was thus little economic basis for social stratification, although there were unquestionably some ecological factors contributing to such dif-ferentiation (for example, the topographical distinction between mountainous and lower-level terrain will have created distinct labour concentrations, and the attendant differences will no doubt have expressed themselves at least to some extent in status differences, resulting in social frictions and disparities).

Settlement Pattern and Social Structure

Likewise, the demographic picture of society, at least in Judah from the eighth century and later, was of a single-centre society (cf. esp. Jamieson-Drake, 1991) with only one important urban centre of concentration of political authority, capital, knowledge, luxury production and artisanship, namely, in succession Lachish (to which, as one must recall, Sennacherib preferred to lay siege, rather than Jerusalem; the latter, being a mere 'royal residence', he simply bottled up – see Pritchard, 1958: 287–8) and then Jerusalem. A similar picture may perhaps have obtained in the quondam northern kingdom of Israel, where the massive fortress and administrative city of Jezreel (cf. Ussishkin and Woodhead, 1997) probably played a major role until it was succeeded by the capital in Samaria (the chronology of this succession is admittedly uncertain). So there will have existed a significant gap between the lifestyles and perspectives of Jerusalemites and those of Judaeans in general, and between the urban wealthy of northern Israel and the common run of rural Israelites. However, given the small size of the respective populations in question and the kinship base of their social organization, one ought not to exaggerate the differences. Those enjoying positions of power and influence at the top of society will seldom have been more than a marriage or two away from those at the very bottom, meaning that there will inevitably have been a large common fund of shared values, beliefs, traditions, attitudes and the like.

Social organisation (cf. esp. Lemche, 1988: 90–104; idem, 1996: 96–108) was apparently structurally based on the clan (*mišpacha*), although it is only infrequently mentioned in the Old Testament, and the patrilineal lineage (*bêt 'ab*), of which the individual components were nuclear families consisting, as a rule, of a husband and a single wife, plus their offspring. The extended, polygamously based family in which several (up to three) generations dwelled together was, however, regarded as the ideal (note the example of Jacob in the Old Testament), although it was, for obvious economic and practical reasons, only rarely realized, as has been the case even up to modern times.

The supraordinate political structure was the tribe (*šæbæt, mattæ*), except in times of strong politically centralized leadership, when there were political and geographically localized subdivisions. At such times, the tribe became submerged beneath imposed structures of government as a sort of reserve ideology (cf. Lemche, 1988: 130–1), available in the event of the collapse of the central power. (Thus, for example, although the Israelite and Judaean tribes had played no political role for many centuries, the apostle Paul was still able to identify himself as a Benjaminite, Phil 3:5.) When centralized, government was usually monarchical, pursuant to the ideal of dynastic succession that prevailed everywhere in the ancient Near East, with the administration of the state conducted largely by the sovereign's extensively ramified kinship group (real and fictive). In rural communities, authority was exercised by the village or town elders (*zeqenim*), one of whom, the local 'big man', probably served as *primus inter pares* or headman.

The Patronage Principle

The ultimate principle of authority permeating both societies was, as in the ancient Near East as a whole, and as has been pointed out, the extensive web of patronage relationships which linked superiors to inferiors everywhere. The relationship between the king and his nobles was one of patron to client group, just as, in village society, the local 'big man' was also in a position to grant land and favours to lower-ranking clients. An obvious example of this in the Hebrew Bible would be Boaz in the book of Ruth. Likewise, when king Saul asks his Benjaminite supporters whether the renegade David 'will give every one of you fields and vineyards . . . make you all commanders of thousands and commanders of hundreds?' (1 Sam 22:7), he is merely reflecting his own role as tribal 'big man' and patron of his courtiers.

Within the nuclear family, the head of the family was patron to those born or bought into and dependent upon the family. Hence, for example, the duty to circumcise 'every male throughout your generations, whether born in your house, or bought with your money from any foreigner who is not of your offspring', Gen 17:12. Similarly, when Laban informs Jacob that, with respect to Jacob's family and offspring, 'The daughters are my daughters, the children are my children, the flocks are my flocks, and all that you see is mine' (Gen 31:43), he is straightforwardly reasserting his rights of patronage over and against the expectations and claims of his dependent (client), Jacob.

The reciprocal social understandings embraced by these patronage relationships and their ramifications are schematically expressed in the Old Testament in the language of covenant, understood as the granting of a charter from superior (patron) to inferior (client). Indeed, a great deal of fascinating theology that was to prove of decisive importance for the early Christian movement is directly predicated on the patronage-covenantal metaphor which adumbrates this relationship in the Hebrew Bible.

Marriage was both endogamous and exogamous, with endogamy retaining the status of ideal. Here Jacob's journey to Paddan Aram in Genesis 28–32 to marry two Aramaic kinswomen is again paradigmatic (see Goody, 1990: 342–60). However, economic and social necessity often compelled exogamy. (For example, a small village society may simply not offer sufficient candidates for the available partners, so that there is no alternative to marrying outside the kinship group. Recourse to marriage within the kinship group in such situations, as is shown by the case of the Samaritans, results in genetic and cultural suicide.)

Finally, there is the issue of language. There is an Aramaic component in two major Biblical books, albeit ones scholars have traditionally assigned to very late times, and Aramaic is well attested, if only in a relatively small number of documents in the Dead Sea Scrolls finds from the vicinity of Khirbet Qumran. Moreover, occasional Aramaic words in the psalms and in prophetic poetry permit the conclusion that at least those who were familiar with the culture underlying the Biblical literature were conversant with, if not fluent in, Aramaic as well as Hebrew.

Moreover, the Hebrew of the Old Testament itself divides into a standard Biblical Hebrew and a so-called 'Late Biblical Hebrew', which, however, cannot be shown to be later than the 'standard' type, as the oldest extant manuscripts, found in the caves in the vicinity of Khirbet Qumran, are all contemporaneous witnesses (on the difficulties of dating the various forms of Hebrew, see Cryer, 1991).

Furthermore, the Hebrew-language documents found in Qumran and in Masada and elsewhere from around the inter-testamental period reveal the existence of: 1 a characteristic 'Qumran Hebrew' (Qimron, 1986), 2 a variety of proto-Mishnaic Hebrew (4QMMT, i.e. the so-called 'Rule of the Works of the Law', and the Copper Scroll) (Morag, 1988), 3 at least two different orthographies (Qumran Hebrew and 'Biblical Hebrew'; cf. Tov, 1986) and, 4 at least two scripts (one based on the Aramaic 'square' script, and one deriving from the Phoenician-based tradition that goes back to pre-exilic times; cf. Cross, 1961). The differences could as easily be accounted for by social or regional distinctions within Syrian-Palestinian society, as by the assumption that texts in so many different types of Hebrew can only be explained in terms of an extensive historical development.

In modern times, the victory of the East Midland dialect of English spoken in London and its environs in the struggle to dominate the development of the English language, and the triumph of the German of the Meissner chancellery over its competitors in Germany, provide good historical examples of the process by which political centrality and importance lead to linguistic dominance. The lack of such a clear linguistic picture in the Dead Sea texts of the Hellenistic-Roman period paints a different picture: as much linguistic diversity as I have described above might be taken to suggest that as late as the times of the collection of documents in the caves in the vicinity of Khirbet Qumran, the region of Judah/Judaea can hardly be claimed to have achieved that measure of ethnic consolidation that usually manifests itself in the emergence of a common, dominant dialect. Indeed, it may have been some such linguistic situation that led to the production of the Dead Sea Scrolls: an attempt to create a national religious literature in the traditional – and endangered – language of the region (i.e. Hebrew).

In short, the societies of ancient Israel and Judah lacked both political cohesion and the sort of linguistic unity that points to the existence of a sense of national identity. This appears to have been the case throughout the history of the region, so that the notion of a great 'Israelite' empire, based on a single people worshipping a single god, may be regarded as a feature of the ideology of the Hebrew Bible rather than a historical reality. A member of the military colony in Elephantine, in Egypt, designates himself *yhdy* (either 'Jew' or 'Judaean') in contracts and the like, but never *yśr'ly* ('Israelite'), and the first Judaean leader who can be shown on the basis of extra-Biblical evidence to have designated himself as a ruler of Israel was first the rebel prince, Simeon bar Kosiba, in the second century AD. Moreover, the 'Israel' bar Kosiba (bar Kochba) speaks of is the camp that was the centre of his rebellion; for him, 'Israel' was a quantity in the making, not a historical reality.

The Common Proprium of Magic and Religion

Social anthropology has attempted since the nineteenth century to maintain a distinction between magic and religion that is only valid to a limited extent. Certainly one of the most prominent characteristics of modern 'primitive', 'savage' or 'traditional' societies (all three terms have been or are in use in contemporary social anthropology to characterize societies with simple material cultures and no written literature) is the central niche occupied by magic in them, as has been evident since the seminal studies of E. E. Evans-Pritchard and others in the 1930s and later. The writer has pointed out elsewhere (Cryer, 1994b: 90–1) that this centrality answers nicely to the centrality of magic in the ancient 'high-cultural' civilizations of India, China, Egypt and Mesopotamia. The strict separation of the two – including the antithesis between them that was claimed by the great Emile Durkheim – seems rather to be a product of the specifically Western historical experience and represents yet another distortion caused by the limitations imposed by our point of view (see above all Cryer, 1994b: 89–92). I think that, in particular, we have been prone to overestimate the importance of writing and written cultural products as criteria for distinguishing complex from 'primitive' societies. The distinctions are far more a matter of social organization and the function of social institutions than of some inherited essence. Religion tends in general to be a collective phenomenon, with the priest as its mediator to the whole society, whereas magic attends more to the needs of the individual in specific situations, who has then a patient–specialist relationship to the magical practitioner. But these are tendencies and are certainly not to be exaggerated. Indeed, one and the same functionary may (and often does) play the roles of both priest and magical specialist in a given society (Cryer, 1994b: 243–50).

The Problem of Definition
(See Tylor, 1958; Frazer, 1911; Mauss and Hubert, 1902–3; Malinowski, 1974; Durkheim, 1976; O'Keefe, 1982; Lewis, 1986)

All historical attempts to define magic have failed seriously, as being either too reductive to cover a significant portion of acknowledged cases, or else being so inclusive as to leave virtually nothing out. The difficulty is that, even within one and the same society, there is no unequivocal understanding of existence such that all phenomena are assigned to a single category by native believers. So, for example, the best hunter in the tribe may fail to make his kill. He may explain the matter himself by invoking magical causation: I was bewitched, and therefore failed. The village priest may instead invoke theological causation: he was impure, so the gods punished him and he accordingly failed. Finally, his rival may have yet a third theory: X is not the great hunter people imagine him to be, which is why he failed; a species of pragmatic causation (I do not say 'empirical' causation, as no magic-using society, or 'magic society', for short, has a concept of strict empiricism which rules out over-determination.). Hence the task of accounting for magic in a given society would entail study of the ways that society itself rubricizes causation in order to account for experience.

However, what magic entails is not merely a way to explain experience; it is also in itself an attempt to act. To attain something by magical action is to obtain it in a way that is distinct from all others. It is a way of reaching a goal that in many cases can only be reached by magic.

Traditionally, there are two provinces of magic, namely magical action and divination. If we examine these from the point of view of external social behaviour, the former may be characterised as 'a set of socially defined and structured procedures for producing in a society what is regarded to be action on the basis of what are presumed to be extra-human sources'. The latter may be characterized very similarly; divination consists of 'a set of socially defined and structured procedures for producing in a society what is regarded to be knowledge on the basis of what are presumed to be extra-human sources'.

Both provinces of magic consist of procedures, as they do not constitute a closed system for dealing with the world. In fact, a magic society is radically open to borrowing new procedures from other societies, as it is always the next spell or ritual that is potentially the most effective, and the dominant ideology in magic societies is that foreign societies X and Y, distant and only dimly acknowledged, have more efficacious magic than does one's own society. The ideal society from which to borrow magic is hence one that no one knows well, as this enables the magician to inscribe the qualities he desires upon the magic in question; and, it must be thought to be powerful in order to justify borrowing its magic.

Now both magical action and magical knowledge are subjectively defined. A conjuration for driving out a sickness demon must 'change the psychological frame' within which the sufferer finds himself and redefine it as a site and context of magical healing. Hence it will recommend a given symbolic understanding of the suffering in question, and it concludes with a statement that, by burning a flock of wool, dissolving a lump of clay, destroying an image of the demon in question or the like, the demon has been expelled or destroyed, and the illness defeated. In other words, as anthropologist Victor Turner has repeatedly emphasized, magic deals with problems which may not be accessible on the real plane, but it does so on an ideal plane, where it dispells them by means of symbolic action. Hence the spell itself is a complex symbolic vehicle which relies on prior social agreements (such as the client–specialist relationship which provides the warrant for the conjuror's actions) which permit the conjuror to redefine the sickness situation in terms of healing. It then pronounces the performative utterance 'you are healed' in one fashion or another.

Similarly, a divinatory act, particularly in the ancient Near East, portrays the supplicant as the plaintiff in a legal case who feels himself wronged and so has applied to the gods to 'judge my case, make my decision'. All questions are essentially only requests for a yes or no verdict; hence the divinatory act simply legitimates (or does not) a given understanding of an actual problem. This sort of consultation also depends on prior social agreements, such as, again, the client–specialist relationship. The forensic understanding of the matter at hand is the symbolic vehicle chosen in order to deal with the problem, and the yes or no which the oracle pronounces is a performative utterance which either legitimates or does away with a given symbolic understanding of the problem in hand. Throughout the ancient Near East, the primary metaphorical understanding of the divinatory situation was of a courtroom (forensic) procedure.

The Production of New Magic

In hierarchically ordered societies there is vastly more magic at the bottom of society than there is at the top. The top level forbids certain kinds of magic, such as, for example, sorcery (i.e. harmful magic) or divination pertaining to the royal succession or the like by any but members of the ruling elite. It is also full of elite disdain for the welter of popular superstition that the masses below advocate. This means, in reality, that new magic enters the society in two ways: a) it is selected by the elite and cultivated from the many types flourishing among the lower levels of society, and b) it is imported from outside the society in question and imposed, as it were, 'from above'. Indeed, magic is frequently and particularly so in the ancient Near East a concern of the learned elite that govern or advise the upper echelons of society.

It is always assumed that magic is efficacious, so that knowledge of magic is regarded as real knowledge, and hence is precious and is reserved for the use of specialists. If the society should happen to be literate, then writing will be a major vehicle of the propagation and preservation of various magics. At the bottom of society, new magic is produced by experimentation and by contact with neighbouring social groups.

Two features are essential to enable the importation of foreign magic: 1 the magic in question must come from a society that is known mainly by hearsay to possess powerful magic, and 2 the specific type of magic is either a parallel to existing forms of magic in the importing society, or else it is wholly foreign, and hence may be 're-inscribed' with new content for domestic purposes by the importing magical specialist. We should note in this connection that the 'distance' of a given society from the magic-borrowing one need not be physical. Purposely delimited ethnic groups, such as the Jews or the Gypsies, traditionally retain sufficient psychological 'distance' from the societies within which they live for high evaluations of their magical prowess easily to flourish in the latter. The same will also be true to some extent of secret societies existing within more open societies; hence the remarkable rumours that have at times existed in various countries about the freemasons, the Jesuits and so forth.

The Role of Stories

The British social anthropologist I. M. Lewis once ruminated as to how it can be that people in magic-using societies persist in using magic in spite of its many failures and the fact that its users seem to be aware that it is not 'what it has been made out to be' (Lewis, 1987: 19). Similarly, the great Polish-British social anthropologist, Bronislaw Malinowski (cf. Cryer, 1994b, 67–70), held that the actual magics he was aware of were strikingly prosaic and undramatic, simple formulae for ensuring a good hunt or a successful fishing expedition, or the like, not awesome conjurations to bring up the long dead or open secret hideouts in sheer granite cliffs to the robber chieftain and his band.

The disparity between magic as practised and magic as it appears in traditional stories about magic use points to the *story* as one of the vehicles of magical praxis in a given society. Magical stories enhance the romance and wonder associated with magic; they may also inspire terror and awe in their readers and hearers. Hence they are essential background elements to that revaluation or re-inscription of any actual use of magic that is the psychological basis of its success, and of the success of other magics. This is why a banal Mesopotamian conjuration against toothache takes its point of departure in the great and wondrous events of the creation of the world, and why such otherwise prosaic ingredients as flour or wool are redefined as *materia magica* (often by specifying that the samples in question be wholly new, that is, never before taken in use in man's world for their conventional purposes, since, being 'virgin', they partake of the pristine quality of new creation) in conjunction with rituals of healing or cleansing. The folk stories about magic provide the imaginative framework which permits a given situation to be redefined as an example of magical healing, cursing, counter-magic, or whatever.

This insight into the role played by magical stories helps us better to understand the folkloristic character of some of the stories about the wonders performed by Moses and Aaron, Balaam's talking ass and the miracles performed by Elijah and Elisha. They show us something of the imaginative backdrop against which the conventionalized magics that were actually in use in ancient Israel and Judah were understood.

Magic and Empiricism

Nothing could be more wrong-headed than to imagine that magic is particularly concerned with the *empirical outcomes* of the magical procedures employed in a given society (see esp. Cryer, 1994b: 42–95). Systems of magical action and divination persisted in the ancient Near East for over two millennia, not because the inhabitants of the region were too stupid to see that magic does not 'work', but because they had a different understanding than we do of in what the efficaciousness of magic consists. One might as appositely ask why contemporary physicians routinely prescribe one or another course of chemotherapy for certain carcinomas, well knowing that the statistical evidence shows this course of action to be useless in such cases: society must do its utmost, the physician must act, and he is not perceived as having acted (not even by himself) unless he has prescribed the most powerful treatment available. Of course, the attending physician may rationalize his behaviour in such a situation with the argument that he must strengthen the patient's 'will to live', or whatever, but this is basically an appeal to a non-empirical category. I offer this observation merely to point out that also science or, rather, scientism, is occasionally the object of magical use even in supposedly empirically orientated societies. No one is astonished in contemporary western society when a sufferer dies in such circumstances; nor are they in 'traditional' societies when the prescribed magical remedy fails. Everybody dies; in fact, it is only in Western societies, where we isolate the dying from the rest of society, that death is regarded as an unnatural outcome. This is not to say, however, that society must acquiesce in death. Society must at least try to defend its members, and magical healing procedures are part of the effort in which society can be seen to be trying its utmost. It is essential that a society understand itself as having done its best in both cases; and no society known to me confesses failure in advance of treatment. In fact, to do so would be equivalent to a confession of anomie, of a society's inability to present the world to its members in an intelligible manner, leading to their surrender to meaninglessness and hopelessness. (On the function of cultural institutions as providing meaning see Hanson, 1975.)

The Biblical Understandings of Magic
(cf. Guillaume, 1938; Ehrlich, 1953; Witton Davies, 1898; Jirku, 1913; Cryer, 1994b; Jeffers, 1998)

Since, as we have seen, there is a great disparity between the historical world that archaeology and extra-Biblical inscriptions allow us to glimpse and the Biblical self-understandings of magical phenomena, it will be necessary to present briefly the Old Testament understanding of magic on its own terms.

The Old Testament sketches out brief origin traditions for many aspects of human existence: man's right to eat plants (Gen 1:3) and animals (Gen 9:3), his wearing of clothing (Gen 3:21), the founding of the first city (Gen 4:17), the origin of small-cattle nomadism (Gen 4:20), the origin of musical instruments (Gen 4:21), the craft of the blacksmith (Gen 4:22), man's ethnic and national distinctions (Gen 10:1ff.), the origin of the languages of the world (Gen 11:1–9) and much besides. However, the various forms of magic are simply presupposed as existing and familiar aspects of human existence. Thus, for example, when, as far back as in the 'patriarchal period' Isaac's wife Rebecca experiences odd signs in connection with her pregnancy, she automatically consults an undefined type of oracle which predicts the birth of twins who will struggle for mastery over each other (Gen 25:22–6). Later, her son Jacob experiences a reliable dream revelation while spending the night at the site of the later sanctuary of Bethel (Gen 28:10–17), and his son Joseph's skills as both mantic dreamer and dream interpreter (Gen 37:5–11; 40–1) are well known. Moreover, the texts are also well aware that such non-Israelites as a Philistine king (Gen 20:1–7) and an Egyptian pharaoh (Gen 41:1–8, 17–24) can receive in their sleep both reliable direct messages and portentous dreams which require interpretation.

Active magic is demonstrated by Moses and, on occasion, Aaron, who prevail over the best efforts of Pharaoh's wise men through a series of great and terrible wonders (Exod 7–11). Furthermore, much of the legislation in the purity laws contains echoes and reverberations of magical ritual known elsewhere. There is a straightforward subtext to both the interpretive activity of Joseph and the Mosaic thaumaturgy, as well as Daniel's efforts: Israelite divination and magic, respectively, are superior to that of the specialists of the great courts of the ancient Near East. Indeed, reflecting Yahwistic universalism, when the Philistine diviners enquire as to the cause of a plague that has ravaged their cities, they are told that it is the god of Israel (1 Sam 6:1–16) (on Philistine divination see Garbini, 1997: 216–21). Likewise, the Balaam narrative (Num 22–4) suffices to show that neither foreign sorcery nor foreign divination avails against Israel.

Furthermore, the episode of the flowering of Aaron's staff (Num 17) and the deaths of the sons of Korah (explicitly characterized as a wonder in answer to a divinatory enquiry: Num 16:27–33) shows that Israelite magic was understood as subserving and prototypically bolstering the authority of the religious hierarchy. In furtherance of this, both Israelite magic and divination are embedded within an explicitly theological framework: Joseph does not himself claim to interpret dreams; rather, as he says, 'interpretations belong to God' (Gen 40:8), just as the episode in which Moses smites the rock (Num 20:10–13) shows that Moses's power is merely on loan from the deity. Here, as elsewhere in the ancient East, magic figures as a manifestation of the official religion. This view must be urged virtually in the teeth of traditional interpretations of magic in ancient Israel and Judah, which regard magic as a foreign intrusion into what has been held to be the first monotheistic society (see esp. Blau, 1898).

This acknowledgement prompts yet another insight, namely that the prohibition on magic and divination in the Old Testament (e.g., Lev 19:26; Deut 18:10–14) is not a blanket condemnation of these practices, but a condemnation of practices that are not under the control of the religious hierarchy and which do not subserve the official ideology (cf. Cryer, 1994b: 324–7). Saul did not, for example, chase the diviners out of Israel because there was anything inherently wrong with diviners, but because he sought to obtain control over the means of revelation. When it suited his purposes, he was perfectly content to avail himself of the services of a 'mistress of an *'ob'* (1 Sam 28; on necromancy in ancient Israel and Judah see Tropper, 1989). As in other both primitive and modern societies, divination reflects existing relationships of power and status (Cryer, 1994b, 326–9).

The Evolutionary Picture

The Old Testament works in a number of ways with a retrospective view of how things functioned 'in the old days', a view that tacitly implies that this is not how things are 'now' – that is, the 'now' of the notional narrator. Thus, for example, it knows of a time when men did not live by the sweat of their brows, or women reproduce in pain, and when the earth did not begrudge man its produce (Gen 3:17–19), and men all worked together on common projects because they spoke the same language and dwelled in the same place (Gen 11:1–9), when men lived vast spans of years (e.g. Gen 5), and the like. There are even signs of a certain degree of development: God's revelation to Israel on Sinai (Exod 20–3) is supplemented by extensive bodies of legislation in the main body of the Pentateuch; the Danites, originally sited in Philistine territory (Judg 13–16) relocate to north of the Sea of Chinnereth (Judg 17–18). Likewise, the time of the judges gives way to the period of the monarchy, which itself witnesses the change from united to dual monarchy (1 Kgs 11–12), ruling dynasty (Saulide to Davidide and, in the later northern kingdom, a staccato succession of new lines worthy of a banana republic), battle customs (1 Sam 30:21–5), the clothing of the royal daughters (2 Sam 13:18), and much besides. Even individuals change in the Old Testament narratives: Joab, the nephew and later general of the young David, goes grey-haired to his grave (1 Kgs 2:6), and David himself declines from the confident young stripling who has fought with bears and lions (1 Sam 17:34–5) to the withered dotard who lay in the arms of the beautiful Shunammite Abishag, and 'knew her not' (1 Kgs 1:1–4).

It is accordingly interesting to observe that the Old Testament includes the means of the divine revelation within this evolutionary history. In the garden of Eden, man and God speak face to face with one another (Gen 3). Afterwards, however, revelation is often through dreams (Gen 15:12ff.; Gen 28:10–17) or mediated by angels (Gen 16:7ff.; 18–19; 21:17ff.; 22:11ff., etc.), with the sole exception of the revelation vouchsafed to Moses, the only man in the history of salvation with whom God speaks 'face to face' (Exod 33:11; Num 12:7–8; Deut 5:4–5, etc.).

There is a fundamental ambiguity here from which we can learn a fair amount. Aaron is at one juncture termed the 'prophet' of Moses (Exod 7:1). Abraham, too, is called 'prophet' on a single occasion (Gen 20:7). The framework of the book of Deuteronomy, however, insists that, since the death of Moses, 'there has not arisen a prophet since in Israel like Moses, whom the Lord knew face to face, none like him for all the signs and wonders which the Lord sent him to do in the land of Egypt' (Deut 34:10–11). On the Deuteronomic understanding, then, prophecy is valid revelation, but it cannot compete in many respects with the prophetic revelation bequeathed to Moses. This is yet another example of the Old Testament recollection of a distant golden past, when things were better than they are now.

Prophecy is also far and away the leading means of revelation in the chronographic works in the Old Testament which relate the fortunes of the land from the conquest onwards. Thus already Saul is salved (1 Sam 10:1) as king by Samuel the 'seer' (*chozæ*), which is explained (1 Sam 9:9) as being the same thing as a 'prophet' (*nabî*). For his part, David is also salved by Samuel (1 Sam 16:1ff.), and has all of two court prophets, Gad (1 Sam 22:5; 2 Sam 24:11ff.) and Nathan (2 Sam 7; 2 Sam 12:1–14; 1 Kgs 1:11–40). Moreover, the breakup of David's storied empire is encouraged by the prophet Ahiah of Shiloh (1 Kgs 11:29–40). A nameless 'man of God' who is also designated 'prophet' by a colleague (1 Kgs 13:18) predicts the destruction of the 'illicit' altar in Bethel (1 Kgs 13:1ff.) by the future good king Josiah (from the point of view of the books of Kings, no altar outside of Jerusalem is legitimate). Yet another prophet predicts the destruction of the north Israelite king Baasha (1 Kgs 16:1–4), and an entire cycle of stories records the fortunes of the Israelite prophets Elijah and Elisha (1 Kgs 17–18; 21:17–24; 2 Kgs 1–9; 13:14–21). 1 Kgs 22 records that the death of the evil king Ahab, husband of the foreign Jezebel, was predicted by the prophet Micaiah ben Imlah (1 Kgs 22:19–23). Indeed, in a retrospective of the career of the erstwhile northern kingdom the narrator notes that 'the Lord warned Israel and Judah by every prophet and every seer, saying, "Turn from your evil ways".' (2 Kgs 17:13). Later, the prophet Isaiah promises king Hezekiah deliverance from the siege of Sennacherib (2 Kgs 19:20ff.), just as the prophet Jeremiah, although not mentioned in Kings, is said in Chronicles (2 Chron 36:12, 21–2) and the book of Jeremiah (esp. chs 7 and 26) to have been active and even to have played a major role during the Babylonian siege and conquest of Jerusalem.

The chronographic literature records only a little about prophecy during the post-exilic period. However, the superscriptions in the book of Ezekiel define this prophet as one of those who went into exile already during the first Babylonian incursion, i.e. in *c.* 597 BCE), and the book bearing his name contains many oracles localized to specific sites in Babylon. Also, the books of Haggai and Zechariah are supposed to be collections of oracles by post-exilic prophets who aided Ezra and Nehemiah in the work of restoration. Furthermore, the book of Nehemiah records that Nehemiah's enemies charge that he had set up prophets to proclaim himself king (6:7) (an interesting testimony to the well-known use of official divination to provide divine validation for political measures that lack other forms of validation), and a false prophet named Shemaiah ben Delaiah prophesies that there is a plot against Nehemiah's life (6:10–12).

Finally, an oracle in the last chapters of Zechariah (13:2–6), which are generally held to be quite late, regards it as essential to the restoration of the land that it be purified of all prophets; then 'if any one again appears as a prophet, his father and mother who bore him will say to him "You shall not live, for you speak lies in the name of the Lord" '(v 3).

The last passage has given rise to a certain tradition to the effect that prophecy ceased in the post-exilic period, a claim that can derive some legitimacy from the fact that the collection of Dead Sea scrolls in the caves near Khirbet Qumran do not number any prophets otherwise unknown to us, although they do contain a fair amount of previously unknown apocalyptic and other literature. Likewise, although Flavius Josephus does know of itinerant prophets in his own time, he knows nothing of literary activity by any of them, nor of any past writing prophets unknown to us.

On the other hand, there is a nascent tendency in Qumran to interpret certain psalms as prophetic works by composing special interpretive keys (so-called 'pesharim', interpretations; see 4Q171 and 173) identical to those which were produced for the works of some of the prophets. This may have been a step in the expansion of the prophetic corpus, at least in Qumran. It is not difficult to imagine one or more psalms becoming grouped together by appropriate editing under the name of some legendary figure.

In other words, even without paying more than cursory attention to the three major prophets Isaiah, Jeremiah and Ezekiel, or to the lesser collection of the twelve, it is clear that the Old Testament understands the primary mode of Yahweh's self-revelation to his people as prophecy. There is also a recurrent theme in Israel and Judah's past-referring traditions to the effect that prophecy had either stopped completely in late post-exilic times, or else that it had changed character and become degenerate.

There have naturally been no end of attempts to bring the phenomenon of prophecy as such within the compass of the history of religions and the phenomenology of studies of religions, and to accommodate it to the Old Testament understanding of historical development. These approaches have concentrated to a significant extent on comparisons with various forms of ecstatic prophecy (cf. e.g. Hölscher, 1914; Haldar, 1945), as these have manifested themselves historically in the ancient Near East in general. This discussion has been modified to some extent by a growing awareness among scholars that the introduction of the concept of 'ecstasy' does not solve any problems. It is unclear how the extreme forms of psychologically "ecstatic" states (such as would seem to be represented by the ravings of the 70 elders in Num 11:24–30, or of Saul and the prophets in 1 Sam 19:18–24) could result in such carefully composed collections as the Israelite and Judaean prophetic works. The discussion has gained a good deal of nuance thanks to the publication of a fair amount of 'prophetic' material deriving from the Old Babylonian-period city-state of Mari, on the upper Euphrates, which has shown that there, too, 'prophecy' was a differentiated phenomenon which actually embraced a variety of events ranging from unintelligible ecstatic states to dream reports, speech omens and other forms of concrete oracles (Moran, 1969: 15–56; Noort, 1977).

From a social-anthropological point of view, the discussion has gained greatly in nuance thanks to comparisons with the very widely attested phenomenon of shamanism, as magisterially defined by the late Mircea Eliade (Eliade, 1951; Widengren, 1969).

It should be noted that attempts to relate Israelite and Judaean prophecy to historically and empirically attested psycho-social phenomena fail to do justice to the purely *literary* characterization of prophecy in the Old Testament. Here, as I have indicated, the overwhelming tendency is to represent prophecy as the 'Israelite' mode of contact with Yahweh par excellence. It was not, however, the only means of such contact, as we shall see presently.

Pseudo-evolution: The Tradition of 'Priestly' Divination
(see Cryer, 1991; 1994b: 286–305; Küchler, 1919; Begrich, 1934)

Having sketched out the internal Old Testament understanding of the history of revelation, it must be added that the tradition also records a revelation that was mediated through one or more 'technical' means of divination, starting with the gift of the Urim and Thummim to the tribe of Levi in Deut 33:8 and ending, at least apparently, just before David installed the Ark of the Covenant in Jerusalem (2 Sam 5:19, 23–4. There are several such oracles throughout the career of David; this is the last of them). Numerous scholars in past times have believed this course of development to reflect a historical transition from 'priestly' to 'prophetic' divination in ancient Israel (cf., e.g., Begrich, 1934; Guillaume, 1938). The implication is that, with the holy city in the possession of the Davidic dynasty and the Ark installed there, revelation can now proceed through the mediation of the court prophets; and in truth, we hear only of discussions between kings and prophets, whether 'court prophets' or not, in the rest of the Hebrew Bible.

i have argued elsewhere (Cryer, 1994b: 286–95) that this evolution is entirely schematic and bears no relation to any actual historical development. In point of fact, the Old Testament continues to make reference to many forms of divination and presupposes that its audience was familiar with them.

Other Forms of Divination than Prophecy
(see esp. Cryer, 1994b: 229–323; Jeffers, 1998)

The ambiguity I alluded to above consists in the fact that the Old Testament makes no overt attempt to conceal the fact that other sorts of magical divining were going on among the Israelites. Already in Deut 33:8–10, the so-called 'Blessing of Moses', Moses asks the Lord to bestow his Urim and Thummim on Levi, whose job is further specified as teaching Israel the Law and administering the sacrifices. A number of passages, but above all the Greek version (the Septuagint, or LXX) of 1 Sam 14 (esp. v 41) allow us to suppose that the Urim and Thummim are sacred lots of some sort, as many scholars have held. However, in reality, it is precisely 1 Sam 14 that rules out the possibility that they are lots, as we are told that the priest who is administering the oracle in question was unable to obtain a valid response for an entire day (v 37). This suggests that 'Urim and Thummim' are two types of oracular responses, rather than specific sorts of lots or counters, as it is patently impossible in a manner of speaking to flip a coin and arrive at no result for an entire day, and there is no indication that the passage in Samuel intends to be satirical. There were a number of types of divination employed in the ancient Near East which required extensive preparation to obtain a simple yes or no answer, some of which also allowed for the possibility of recording that the omen in question was unclear. Hence I suggest that the reference here is to one of them: possibly, as I have suggested elsewhere, we have to do with the rite of the omen sacrifice or extispicy, as it could only be performed – at most – twice a day. Moreover, at least in Babylon and Assyria, one of the terms for the omen sacrifice was the 'touch (*lipit*) of the hand (*qati*)', a euphemism for stretching out the hand to slaughter the animal in question. At all events, no matter how they are understood, the Urim and Thummim are attested inner-Biblically from the period of the wilderness wanderings until a brief reference in Neh 7:64–5, during the 'post-exilic' period, when we are told that a divine ruling as to whether certain families are to be excluded from the priesthood has to wait 'until a priest with Urim and Thummim should arise' (v 65). This remark has often been taken to suggest that in fact knowledge of how to administer the Urim and Thummim no longer existed in the post-exilic period. But, of course, this conclusion does not follow; it may be that the non-recorded ruling of the Urim and Thummim was simply that the families in question were not to be enrolled among the priests, in which case there was no reason to change existing genealogies or the like. But what the passages mentioned above permit us to conclude is that the Old Testament speaks of a variety of divination administered by 'Levi', that is, by the priestly class, just as Neh 7:65 speaks of a 'priest' (*kohen*) as administrator; it furthermore suggests that this type of divination was in use for many centuries in 'Israel'.

We have already seen that the Old Testament straightforwardly accepts that dreams are valid bearers of information for both Israelites and non-Israelites. Unlike the Urim and Thummim oracle, however, nothing connects the interpretation of dreams specifically with the priesthood. Other forms of divination are presupposed as well, however, as being entirely familiar to 'Israel'. One of the simplest of these is the lot. It is sometimes claimed by apologists who prefer the nineteenth-century view, according to which 'Israel' did not practise magic in any of its forms, that lot-casting was a purely 'secular' activity, unrelated to the cultic sphere. This notion, however, founders on the difficulty that it is unlikely that we can postulate the existence of secularized conceptions of 'randomnicity' prior to the seventeeth or eighteenth centuries AD. It is of a piece with this observation that we read in the Old Testament (Prov 16:33) 'the lot is cast into the lap/but all its counsel is from Yahweh'. In a magic society, there is no uncaused behaviour (nor is there, for that matter, in a strictly Newtonian universe of discourse); in fact, behaviour will frequently be overdetermined, as having both a 'pragmatic' cause and a magical or religious one. (For example, a man might be crushed by a falling tree. The fall of the tree is the pragmatic cause, but the reason it fell just when he was walking by may be regarded as the result of the divine will, or the effects of sorcery, or the result of the victim's own cultic impurity or the like.) Lot-casting, then, like that which apportions the land among the tribes of 'Israel' (Jos 13–19), results in Jonah being pitched into the sea (Jo 1:1–15), and selects Achan for death (Jos 7:16–26) or Saul for the kingship (1 Sam 10:17–24), was clearly regarded as an expression of the divine will.

However, there is reference to a priest undertaking the lot-casting procedure in only a single, if important instance: the apportionment of the conquered lands, and even in this event he does so together with the civil and military leader (i.e. Joshua; see

Jos 14:1; cf. 19:51). So it might be wisest to conclude that lot-casting was a magical activity that could be engaged in by all participants in society, from low and magically unskilled to high and magically sophisticated. Since magic is regarded as valid knowledge in magic societies, and, further, since the channels of knowledge in a given society tend to agree with existing power and status relationships, we may assume without further enquiry that the conclusions of the priest's lot-casting were regarded as more reliable than were those of people in lower echelons of society. In ancient Mesopotamia, by way of comparison, the conclusions of provincial diviners were sometimes sent to the capital to be subjected to the test of the great king's specialists in extispicy, and among the Azande of the Sudan in modern times most males were permitted to use the ultimate divining resource of the poison oracle, but the highest instance available was the poison oracle administered by the prince (cf. Evans-Pritchard, 1980: 162).

The latter observation brings us back to the Urim and Thummim. We have seen that the administration of the Urim and Thummim is regarded in the Old Testament as the pre-eminent priestly form of divination. However, I pointed above to the possibility that 'Urim and Thummim' were simply two different types of oracular response. Combining this observation with the previously described priestly participation in lot-casting, it is accordingly possible that 'Urim and Thummim' simply applies to all or most types of divination. These are ordinarily regarded as efficacious in the Old Testament, but exceptionally so when a priest figures in the role of celebrant.

Outside of prophets, dream interpretation and the Urim and Thummim, the Old Testament speaks of the *teraphim* in a number of contexts (Hos 3:4; Ezek 21:21; Zech 10:2) as oracular instruments. Elsewhere, however, we find reference to them as portable idols (Gen 31:19, 34–5), or even as approximately human-sized idols (1 Sam 19:13, 16). Since the function of an idol is to represent a deity, and since many forms of divination in the Old Testament take place 'in the presence of' the deity, it is possible that the former type merely imply some unspecified variety of divination that was performed in the presence of an idol. The same consideration applies to a scattered selection of passages which speak of divination taking place in the presence of the Ark of the covenant (Num 12:4–6; 1 Sam 3:3–4; 1 Sam 14:18–19). A similar ambiguity arises in conjunction with the mysterious ephod, which is sometimes referred to as a garment (1 Sam 2:18; 2 Sam 6:14), sometimes as part of the high-priestly insignia (Exod 28), and is sometimes mentioned in conjunction with the giving of oracles (1 Sam 14:3; 21:10; 22:18; 23:6, 9; 30:7, etc.).

I have argued elsewhere (Cryer, 1994b, 277–82) that this 'ephod' in fact represents the ornate garment that was used to enclothe representative images of deities in ancient Near Eastern societies, and which itself reflected garments worn by the higher priesthood and the monarch. Hence the Old Testament references to divination in connection with the ephod are possibly also simply references to unspecified forms of divination that required some symbolic representation of the presence of the deity for their performance, as was entirely common in other forms of divination in the ancient Near East.

'Urim and Thummim', then, seem to have been two types of oracular answers which could have been produced by any number of divinatory procedures; this would explain why they are regarded as the special property of the priestly tribe of Levi in Deut 33:8, as priestly divination no doubt represents the Old Testament understanding of elite, socially warranted divination – the summit of divinatory practices with which the inhabitants of ancient Syria-Palestine must have been familiar. In conjunction with most such procedures, some form of symbolic representation of the deity was essential, and the Old Testament is aware of a variety of cultic equipment (the Ark, the teraphim, the ephod) capable of performing this task.

That the Old Testament envisages a hierarchy of types of divination seems indisputable. I have pointed above to the pride of place in much of the literary tradition that was accorded to prophecy (here the prooftext would have to be the presentation of the 'Book of the Law' found by high priest Hilkiah and Shaphan, the scribe, to the prophetess Huldah for validation, 2 Kgs 22:10–20). I have also indicated that divination performed by priests who serve as advisors to the whole society, as in the lot-casting in Shiloh (Josh 9–13), or for the monarchy, as in 1 Sam 14, enjoyed great prestige and is presupposed by the Old Testament narrative traditions about Israel's past. However, divination is also available to lesser lights in society, without priestly or prophetic intermediation.

Thus, for example, Saul's son Jonathan specifies a particular kind of oracle dependent on the verbal responses of the Philistines he and his armour-bearer are preparing to attack ('If they say to us, "Wait until we come to you", then we will stand still in our place and we will not go up to them. But if they say "Come up to us", then we will go up; for YHWH will have given them into our hand. This shall be the *sign* to us' – 1 Sam 14:9–10).

This form of oracle, based on speech, was known throughout the ancient world, from Sumeria (where it was termed *enim.gar*) to Assyria and Babylonia (where it was called an *egirru* omen) to ancient Greece (where it was termed a *kledon*) (see above all Oppenheim, 1956; Cryer, 1994b: 160–1). It might be objected that Jonathan is Saul's crown prince and hence exceptionally privileged with respect to mantic information. However, there are numerous other examples of speech and sound omens in the Old Testament (e.g. as when Gideon is told that something he is about to hear will convince him to attack the Amalekites, Judg 7:10–11: 'shall go down to the camp with Purah, your servant, and you shall hear what they say, and afterwards your hands will be strengthened'; or as when Elisha's former servant, Gehazi, is relating how his master had restored a dead boy to life, and then, as if by coincidence, the resurrected boy's mother comes to plead before the king on an unrelated errand: 2 Kgs 8:4–5. In magical thinking, there is no such thing as coincidence). The speech omen, then, was the common property of all levels of society in ancient Israel and Judah, as it was elsewhere in the ancient world.

The same considerations obviously apply to dream omens since, as was noted above, people at all levels of society, both in Israel and Judah and in the greater world around them, enjoyed the benefit of ominous dreams bearing legitimate information (e.g. Judg 7:13–14, where the dreamer is an Amalekite soldier; Gen 37:5–11, where the dreamer is Joseph, an Israelite shepherd; Gen 41:1ff., where the dreamer is mighty Pharaoh).

It must be emphasized, however, that no matter what its social status, divination was subjected to the controlling strictures of the religious hierarchy. Thus Deut 13 informs us that

> if a prophet arises among you, or a dreamer of dreams, and gives you a sign or a wonder, and the sign or wonder which he tells you comes to pass, and if he says 'let us go after other gods', which you have not known, 'and let us serve them', you shall not listen to the words of that prophet or to that dreamer of dreams . . . that prophet or dreamer of dreams shall be put to death. (Deut 13:1–5)

In other words, no matter what the validity of an omen or oracle might prove to be, the overriding concerns of the religious authority take precedence, and the sanctions it is prepared to impose to ensure its hold on the 'right' source of revelation (i.e. Yahweh) are draconian.

Furthermore, divination in the Old Testament is depicted as subserving not only the cult of Yahweh, but also the political sanction of the crown. The youthful David, on the run from envious king Saul, seeks bread and a weapon from the sanctuary of the 'city of the priests', Nob (1 Sam 21–2). The chief priest, however, also undertakes to 'enquire of Yahweh' on David's behalf (1 Sam 22:10, 13, 15), for which reason Saul orders the entire town slaughtered (cf. v 19). As in primitive societies in general, access to 'knowledge' was strictly limited to those who enjoyed both sufficient social and religious status. It is in conjunction with the slaughter of Nob that we should understand Saul's ban on other forms of divination, including his own attempt to seek recourse to one of the forms he is said to have expelled, when he visits the 'mistress of an *'ob'* in Endor: this simply exemplifies the insistence of the crown on maintaining control of all forms of divination. It differs in detail, but not in essence, from strictures on divination that were utilized in ancient Mari and in the Neo-Assyrian empire and elsewhere (cf. Cryer, 1994b, 326–7).

The Old Testament is therefore aware that a wide variety of forms of divination were employed in ancient Israel and Judah, and that they constituted a hierarchy ranging from the socially warranted forms of priestly and prophetically mediated divination (to the extent that these actually differed from each other) down to those which were freely granted to all members of society, and which accordingly no doubt enjoyed lesser authority in the actual societies of Israel and Judah. Some of these more accessible forms of divination are scarcely mentioned in the Old Testament, except to forbid them (see the list of forbidden types of magic in Deut 18:10–14). I take these to indicate the insistence of the central institutions of cult and state on maintaining control over the means of revelation.

The Role of Women in Israelite and Judaean Magic

An interesting question arises in this connection as to the role of women in conjunction with Israelite and Judaean divination. The Old Testament knows of only a very few prophetesses, such as Deborah (Judg 4:4) and Huldah (2 Kgs 22:14–20), and indeed presents only a single oracle purporting to derive from one of them (Huldah; it is doubtful whether Deborah's song in Judg 5 can be classified as an oracle). When we add to this the fact that the 'mistress of an *'ob'* (a much-discussed term whose precise meaning still eludes us) who is consulted by Saul in order to converse with the ghost of Samuel (1 Sam 28:1ff.) is one of the very diviners forbidden by Saul, it seems as if women's access to the role of divinatory intermediator was severely limited in the society envisaged by the authors of the Old Testament. This is ultimately unsurprising, in that divination in the Old Testament is explicitly subordinated, as we have seen, to the strictures of the religious hierarchy, and the minor role played by women in divination is thoroughly consistent, when we consider the diminutive role according to the Old Testament played by female personnel in the cult as a whole.

It might be added that the modest role played by female diviners and magicians in the societies envisioned by the Old Testament does not appear to leave room for 'possession cults'. The latter frequently take the form of spirit mediumistic movements that empower women in oppressive societies when they seemingly fall prey to the attacks of hostile spirits. Their illnesses require lengthy and expensive courses of treatment, which helps the women to reassert some measure of status in the confrontation with their husbands. The phenomenon has been extensively studied by I. M. Lewis, of London University (Lewis, 1971).

The most despised form of magical enquiry mentioned in the Old Testament is astrology. It is savagely attacked by the so-called Second Isaiah, who challenges the Babylonians to

> Stand fast in your enchantments and your many sorceries with which you have laboured from your youth . . . You are wearied with your many counsels; let them stand forth and save you, those who divide the heavens, who gaze at the stars, who at the new moons predict what shall befall you. Behold they are like stubble, the fire consumes them, they cannot deliver themselves from the power of the flame (Isa 47:12–14)

Similarly, a passage in Jeremiah remonstrates with the Israelites, that they

> Learn not the way of the nations, nor be dismayed at the signs of the heavens because the nations are dismayed at them, for the customs of the peoples are false (Jer 10:2)

This is of a piece with a prose addition to the book of Amos which announces that Israel will go into exile because the land is adopting astral deities, termed Sakkuth and Kaiwan (Amos 5:26). This bit of theological redaction thus equates the resort to astrology with the worship of foreign deities. It should be mentioned in this connection that Babylonian and Assyrian astrology shows some signs of being connected with astral cults (Reiner, 1995).

In reality, however, it was impossible for the ancient kindoms of Israel and Judah to practise astrology as it was practised by the Assyrians of the Neo-Assyrian empire, and as it was presumably practised in Babylonia as well (we are not as well informed on this issue, but at least some specialist observers were responsible for the production of the Babylonian 'astronomical diaries' which have been published recently). In Assyria, there was an extensive net of observers in the major provinces of the empire, all of whom reported to the crown when astral phenomena were observed which portended important events for the empire and/or the crown. Moreover, there were extensive series of astronomical observations which enabled these Assyrian scholar–priests to study the skies and recognize anomalies when they observed them (only anomalies were regarded as information-bearing). But the use of such materials presupposes a great deal of pragmatic knowledge about astronomy, as well as practical training in the use of the great series of omens based on heavenly phenomena, as well as such mundane phenomena as earthquakes, flashes of lightning and the like.

It should be obvious that the mini-states of ancient Israel and Judah, based as they were on subsistence economies which provided scarcely sufficient revenues even to provide adequately for their defence, could hardly provide the requisite network of scholar–priests to man such a system. Of course, as the societies underlying the Old Testament lacked the manpower and expertise to practise astrology in any extensive fashion, it is unsurprising that an anti-astrological ideology developed and received literary concretion.

This does not mean that there was no practice of astrology whatsoever in the respective states while they existed, but only that, in the event, astrology in this region will not have been based on observation, but simply on the conclusions of whatever series of handbooks on the subject happened to be available. This would seem to explain why we find in the Aramaic text of 1 Enoch, of which numerous copies were found in the caves of Khirbet Qumran, a so-called 'astronomical section' which lists, among other things, ratios of light to darkness for the days of the year in amounts that are wildly inaccurate, and which, additionally, only account for a single month, rather than a whole year. They were not based on observation, but on someone's inaccurate and schematic calculation. It is a different matter, but not entirely unrelated, that documents from Syria–Palestine (certain calendrical MSS from Qumran; Enoch; Jubilees) show that at least three different calendars were competing with each other in the time around the turn of the millennium. This would not actually have been possible if the Babylonian luni-solar calendar, based on empirical observation, calculation, and periodically corrected, had been in use. Instead, the systems in use appear simply to have been schematically employed, divorced from their observational basis.

Active Magic

Divination is hardly the only form of magic that was practised in the societies of ancient Israel and Judah. Active magic and the defensive arts of the exorcist (which is merely active magic with a negative 'sign', that is, directed against demons and the like) were obviously known in the social world of Syria–Palestine, even if the Old Testament text is reluctant to discuss this aspect of magical usage in 'ancient Israel'. That such phenomena as exorcism and apotropaic magic did exist is amply attested by, for example, parallels between certain provisions in the Old Testament purity legislation and some of the Mesopotamian incantation series, such as Šhurpu, which are designed to protect against a wide range of phenomena (Geller, 1980). I have myself pointed elsewhere to similarities between the Mesopotamian genre of incantations known as *namburbis* and certain of the Old Testament ritual prescriptions, such as, for example the procedures for dealing with cases of suspected 'leprosy' (so called, because true leprosy, caused by Hansen's bacillus, apparently did not exist in the ancient Near East at the time) in Leviticus 17 (Cryer, 1994b: 318–19).

Indeed, having determined from the finds of magical texts from ancient Ugarit that divination was present in widespread fashion in ancient Syria–Palestine, exorcistic is also to be expected, as we find the two paired in a great number of primitive societies, in which divination discovers the magical or religious cause of a complaint, while incantational magic then seeks to redress the difficulty (O'Keefe, 1982, 122–3 and n. 1). A simple example of this procedure in the Old Testament is in the account of king Hezekiah's magical healing by the prophet Isaiah in 2 Kings 20:4–11. This account corresponds well to many magical healing seances in ancient Mesopotamia, as it includes not only divination as to whether the sufferer (king Hezekiah) will recover, but also an account of part of the procedure of his healing (v 7; the account is only partial, as we are not told what prayers or incantations were to accompany the treatment) and a prediction as to the length of time the complaint is expected to last, after which the king will be considered clean (three days) and may re-enter the temple. Similarly, in Assyrian and Babylonian magical medicine, one of the pre-eminent jobs of the diviner–exorcist (Akk. *mašmašu*) was to set a time-limit (Akk. *adannu*) to an illness (see the *CAD*, sub *adannu*; Roberts, 1977).

Of course, the healing and fertility miracles attributed to the prophets Elijah and Elishah (1 Kgs 17:17–24; 2 Kgs 2:19–22; 2 Kgs 4:11–17, 2 Kgs 4:18–37, 2 Kgs 4:38–41, etc.) are couched in the language and metaphor of wonder-working, but neverthe-less record the use of both certain procedures and certain materials (laying the prophet's staff on the mouth of the sufferer, making a poultice of figs, stretching out on the body of the sufferer, throwing such *materia magica* as salt or meal into a contaminated spring or a poisonous repast, and the like) which reveal that not even highly theologically edited texts regard such healing as taking place through the word of God alone. This reflects an awareness that ritual, involving the use of a variety of symbolic components, was also a factor. Moreover, two of the materials used (salt and meal) were staples of the Mesopotamian exorcistic and apotropaic tradition.

Witchcraft, Sorcery and Cursing

As a type of language, a curse is a performative utterance like greeting, promising, marrying, threatening, blessing, instructing, advising and the like: actions which take place, and which can only take place, in and through language. Many societies see no distinction between the efficaciousness of a curse on the level of figurative statement and its realworld realization. Hence it is expected that a curse will kill or have some other unpleasant effect. In anthropological terms, cursing others so that they are struck by misfortune or even death is a variety of sorcery, and when conducted by private individuals this is, of course, a proscribed activity. Hence we find prohibitions on sorcerous practices in both Hammurabi's code (where it is called *kaššaptu*) and in the Old Testament (where it is called by the cognate term, *kešeph*; cf. Deut 18:10).

In some African societies there is a distinction between 'witchcraft', understood as the unconscious harming of one's neighbours by a tribesman with an unacknowledged bent to do so, and 'sorcery', understood as the conscious and malevolent attempt to destroy one's neighbour through purposeful magical action (see above all Evans-Pritchard, 1980; Lewis, 1987: 23–51). The former may be countered through public confrontation and established conflict-resolving procedures. Punishment for the latter is usually draconian and swift. 'Witchcraft' accusations often function in their social context as ways of bringing latent social tensions to expression so that they may be resolved, and in fact a number of studies of 'witchcraft' in Africa have drawn explicit parallels to the ways gossip functions in giving expression to tensions latent within a small society. By contrast, sorcery in African societies is held to be, as in the ancient Near East, a conscious process, and in many societies it is so severely proscribed that no one will even admit to having knowledge of it, much less doing it. In both cases, however, whether notionally conscious or unconscious, the allegation of harmful magic serves the purposes of 'theodicy', in the sense of explaining why something in someone's life has gone wrong: a witch or sorcerer must be at work.

The Evil Eye

Though widely attested in references in rabbinical writings (see Ulmer, 1994), the phenomenon of the evil eye is only directly attested in the Old Testament in a few passages, such as Prov 6: 12–14, which mentions that 'a wicked man goes about with perverted speech, squints with his eyes, drags his feet, points his finger, and makes evil with a corrupted heart'. Conversely, the righteous man is enjoined to 'Let your eyes look straight before you, and your glance be straight' (Prov 4:25). So there is no doubt but that this widespread Near Eastern conception was also understood here. As it is here linked with both speech and pointing the finger, it is clearly understood as a variety of curse (Bryce, 1975).

Witchcraft and Gender

The previously mentioned prohibition of 'witchcraft' in ancient Israelite and Judaean society does not have an immediate address to women, as is the case in other societies, so the witchcraft accusation was probably not one of the mechanisms of social control designed to constrain women's behaviour. No doubt 'witches' and 'sorcerers' could be, at least in theory, either male or female.

In this connection it is worth remarking that, in the entire (relatively compendious) judicial literature of the ancient Near East there is only one known incident in which anyone at all (in this case a woman) is accused through the courts of 'witchcraft', the crime Hammurabi punished with death (Walters, 1970). In the event in question, the case was dismissed by the judges. This perhaps indicates that 'witchcraft' incidents did not ordinarily reach the level of the judicial means of conflict-resolution – and, if they did, they were not necessarily taken all that seriously. This is intelligible, in the sense that the courts will have been administered by the elite of society, whereas witch beliefs are much more likely to have been part of the broad mass of popular beliefs adhered to lower down in ancient Near Eastern and other societies. Hence witch persecution may have been – as is frequently the case today in Africa – a matter of lynch law at the village level. In the Old Testament, the famous 'witch' of Endor (1 Sam 28:1ff.), incidentally, is clearly depicted as one of the divinatory personnel of ancient Israel and Judah; she is nowhere brought into relation with the actual practice of harmful magic, which is to say that she is hardly a 'witch' in a social-anthropological sense at all.

Self-cursing: the Oath

As was the case elsewhere in the ancient Near East, contracts in ancient Israel and Judah were routinely concluded by the utterance of oaths, which may be understood as self-curses, the voluntary taking upon oneself of the consequences attendant upon transgressing against the conditions stated in the transaction in question. Precisely this notion underlies the longer series of consequence clauses in Lev 26:14–40 and Deut 28:15–68, which state in full the curses that will affect 'Israel' if the people transgress against the provisions of the covenant which they have entered into with their god.

In ordinary business transactions, there were lists of human witnesses who might be called into court in the event a contract was broken. But in the event that human witness should prove inadquate to the task, both the leading deity and the reigning king are usually invoked in ancient Mesopotamian contracts, so that the matter is then subject to their jurisdiction. This 'oath of god and king' was clearly also sworn in Syria–Palestine, as a number of passages in the Old Testament reveal (e.g., 1 Kgs 21: 9–13; Prov. 24:21, Isa 8:21, etc.). It would be a serious error to imagine that this sort of self-curse represents a distinction between an appeal to 'secular' authority on the one hand and an invocation of the 'divine' power on the other. After all, the point the scribes found essential to emphasize was that both spheres were invoked side by side, and, hence, that both were essential to catching and punishing an oath-breaker. The implied relationship is one of complementarity, rather than an exclusive either/or (see Cryer, 1994b: 315 n. 2–4). As I have said previously, the coexistence of magic and ordinary daily pragmatic rationality is more complex than one imagines.

Another Self-curse: the Ordeal

No doubt the best example of the self-curse in the Old Testament literature is provided by the ritual of the 'water of bitterness' that is surprisingly well preserved in Num 5:12–31. Here the link between physical symptoms, understood as 'signs' of the divine response to a divinatory enquiry, and the cultic status of the subject of the enquiry, manifested as sickness or health, is made quite explicit.

Verses 12–13 specify that if a woman should be unfaithful to her husband or if he should become jealous of her, then the provisions of the ritual are to be carried out. The double condition prefacing the rite shows that its purpose is thought of as divination, i.e. it will show whether the wife in question has been unfaithful. The means of doing so is, however, a variety of the African poison oracle: the woman takes a self-curse upon her which, if she is innocent, will have no effect, but which, if she is guilty, will 'enter into her and cause bitter pain, and her body shall swell, and her thigh shall fall away' (v 27). Contrariwise, if the woman proves to be innocent, 'then she shall be free and shall conceive children' (v 28). The rite is, then, formally simply a divinatory act yielding a binary answer, like so many others in the ancient Near East. Its obvious parallel in the region is the Mesopotamian ritual of the ordeal, in which a suspected miscreant was bound hand and foot and then thrown into the Euphrates, on the assumption that the gods would rescue him, if innocent, and that they would destroy him, if guilty. Similar magical thinking is present in the seventeenth-century Western European witch test in which the suspected witch was bound and then thrown into a pond. If he or she floated, she was rejected by God's waters, and hence guilty, whereas if she sank, she was accepted, and hence innocent.

In connexion with the ritual in Num 5, many commentators have noted that there is no 'sign' offered as to when the woman is to be set free; she merely is free. Moreover, her subsequent begetting of children only makes sense in a context in which it was assumed that, for theological reasons, no child would come of an unchaste relationship. This assumption is both naive and directly contradicted not only by ordinary experience, but also inner-Biblically by the account of the pregnancy of Bathsheba (2 Sam 11:2–5. One might compare this with an Old Babylonian extispicy omen: 'she will be untrue to her husband and will conceive, [then] saying: may it [the baby] look like him!'); it is likely that the original ritual once had a different ending than is now the case. It is also interesting to note that, although it is only fragmentarily preserved, the pentateuchal witnesses among the Dead Sea Scrolls do not reflect the 'waters of bitterness' ritual at all. In fact, there is altogether much less of the magical and wondrous in the Qumran Pentateuch than is the case with other collections of pentateuchal tradition (e.g. the MT, SP and the LXX) (cf. Cryer, 1998: 98–112). This is perhaps curious in view of the fact that the caves of Qumran actually contained a handful of documents of physiognomical and genethliological (based on birthdates) omens (see 4Q186 and Greenfield and Sokolow, 1989).

The Status of Magic in Ancient Syria–Palestine
As is indicated by the model proposed above for the way new magics arise, magic exists at all levels of any magic-using society. There will be less of it higher up in society, but on the other hand, those magics in use in the higher strata will enjoy the warrants of authority and prestige. Taken as a whole, the ancient Near East took great care to preserve the elite traditions of magic: incantation, adjuration, conjuration, divination and so forth, in written form. This proves to have been the case in ancient

Mesopotamia and Egypt, but also in such remote areas as the quondam Hittite kingdom and the Hurrian kingdom of Mitanni (see esp. Oppenheim, 1977: *passim*; Cryer, 1994b: 124–228). Now magical texts are preserved from ancient Ugarit, and, as I have mentioned, there are a handful among the *c.* 850 documents from the caves of Qumran. However, the numbers in both cases are quite modest, compared with the bulk of other textual materials. This fact is quite striking, given the fact that magical texts comprise the single largest genre of texts preserved elsewhere, with the possible exception of legal texts and records. Hence, in order to account for this disparity, there is reason to ask whether magic played only a) a marginal role in the region, and was of little importance, b) whether it on the contrary enjoyed the very high status of an arcanum, or secret discipline, and so was not on the whole recorded in writing, or c) whether it flourished on the popular level, but received only scant official attention in the literate upper layers of society.

In this connexion the Old Testament witness is of great value, even if it does not directly depict the situation in the ancient societies of Israel and Judah. This is so because the texts nevertheless accord to various forms of magic great social and practical importance; moreoever, they do so in a non-ideological way; they are not trying to persuade us of the importance of certain magics, as is sometimes the case in Mesopotamia (the 'Cuthaean legend of Naram Sin', cf. Gurney, 1955; the 'Advice to a Prince', cf. Lambert, 1960: 110–15). Rather, the high status of magic and divination is simply presupposed as beyond question in such narrations as the account of the dreams of Pharaoh (Gen 37–41) and Nebuchadnezzar (Dan 2; 4). Dividing the land by lot is simply the way to achieve equitable distribution in Josh 13–16. Saul would not dream of going into battle against the Philistines without having secured Yahweh's warrant to do so (1 Sam 14). Moreover, Saul's fall from Yahweh's favour is made manifest by the refusal of the various oracles (prophets, dreams, Urim) to speak to him (1 Sam 28), just as David's ascendant star is underlined by Yahweh's readiness to reply to his enquiries (e.g. 1

Sam 23:2–4; 2 Sam 2:1; 5:19, 22, etc.). And both the Deuteronomistic and Priestly legislative corpora agree that the curses of the covenant will strike Israel down in the event that she fails to keep the covenant.

We can therefore dismiss the first two conjectures presented above (a and b) out of hand: magic in the societies of ancient Syria–Palestine was certainly neither marginal nor a secret of the privileged few. But did it exist wholly or largely on the popular level? There is reason to modify this model, too. In the accounts of Pharaoh's dreams, the narrator has been theologically sophisticated, in that he has taken care to integrate Joseph's magical interpretation of Pharaoh's dreams into the Yahwistic theology, rather than presenting the interpretations as the results of technical or textbook divination. Hence when Pharaoh tells Joseph, 'I have heard it said that when you hear a dream you can interpret it' (Gen 41:15), the latter immediately replies that 'it is not in me. Let God return to Pharaoh a favourable answer' (41:16; note Daniel's similar disclaimer, Dan 2:28–31). Yet the principles Joseph uses in interpreting the dreams exemplify a straightforward symbolism, in which seven ears of corn = seven years, or seven cows = seven years, and the like. This simple exegesis renders the dreams immediately accessible to the lay reader on an uncomplicated and non-technical basis.

By contrast, as I have shown elsewhere, the many seemingly incidental details in the dreams of Pharaoh's wine steward, baker and Pharaoh himself (such as the former grasping Pharaoh's cup in his hand, while the baker has a basket on his head, and the dream of the cows envisions them standing on the banks of the Nile) are all categories of dreamed experiences listed among the sequences of protases listed in an Assyrian 'dream book' that was used in Mesopotamian technical divination (Cryer, 1994b: 267–72; the 'Dream Book' itself has been published in Oppenheim, 1956). Similarly, the monsters in the visions of the book of Daniel seem to have been made of whole cloth, out of the imagination of the writer, but in fact P. A. Porter has shown that their detail derives from collections of Mesopotamian omina based on the births of deformed offspring of domestic animals and, in one series, of people (Porter, 1983; the series itself, known as *šumma izbu*, is published in Leichty, 1970). Such a differentiated use of the magical tradition makes it immediately accessible to the lay audience, while containing depths of detail to which only the literarily sophisticated could respond appropriately.

We may therefore conclude that the audience of the Hebrew Bible comprised a spectrum stretching from the lower echelons to the literarily knowledgeable elite. The lack of written materials of the elite tradition is thus probably the result of the vagaries of preservation of the Israelite and Judaean written tradition as a whole. There is, however, one important point to recall in this connection, namely that the primary form of Israelite and Judaean divination, namely prophecy, has managed to be well preserved, as much of the record of it comprises part of the religio-literary tradition that is recorded in the Biblical texts themselves.

The Practitioners

It cannot be ruled out that the Israelite and Judaean prophets made use of the standard 'technical' means of divination that were the common property of the ancient Orient (as was argued already by Biç, 1951), and indeed many of the forms of, for example, Mesopotamian divination, can be shown to underlie many Biblical references (Cryer, 1994b: 229–324). This suggests that the lore of the Babylonian-Assyrian divining priest (*baru*) and specialist in conjuration (*mašmašu*) was available during the period when the Biblical texts were being developed. This does not help us to fix a date, however, as the Mesopotamian divinatory tradition continued to be passed on in Akkadian well into the Seleucid period (McEwan, 1981).

Furthermore, it is unclear whether priest and prophet were ever understood as separate classes of individuals each with his own mode of legitimacy. The superscriptions to the books of both Jeremiah and Ezekiel imply that their protagonists came from priestly lineage. On the other hand, many of the magics in the Hebrew Bible seem to presuppose that it was possible for ordinary people to administer them, although this naturally loses some of its force when we consider that it might represent Pharisaic 'democratisation' of the tradition.

Some texts suggest that certain types of magic were practised by everyone in the society. There is no reason to reject the imputation in principle. Contrariwise, there is absolutely no reason to assign a wide range of functions to the many gradations of practitioners mentioned in the Old Testament. A subsistence economy does not provide ideal presuppositions for a hugely developed beaucracy, and there will in any case have been numerous overlapping functional roles performed by many ordinary members of such a society (Cryer, 1994b: 246–9). Among the Azande of the Sudan, even ordinary citizens are able to use a wide variety of magical procedures without ceasing to be gardeners, potters, householders or whatever. As in other magic-using societies, those of Israel and Judah used magic both extensively and routinely, but before we shall be able to talk about their respective divinatory traditions in detail we shall have to have the aid of new text finds, preferably including some of the protocols of Israelite and Judaean diviners, or some of the rituals of their exorcists. It would seem a lot to ask, but such finds are otherwise commonplace in the ancient Near East. The find of a few letters illustrating popular attitudes towards magical practices would naturally also be helpful. For the present, however, we shall have to confine ourselves to largely theoretical observations, based on comparative data, such as those offered here.

ABBREVIATIONS

ABL   Robert Francis Harper, *Assyrian and Babylonian Letters Belonging to the Kouyunjik Collection of the British Museum*, vols 1–14, London, Chicago 1892–1914.

ABRT   James Alexander Craig, *Assyrian and Babylonian Religious Texts*, vol. I, Leipzig, 1895; vol. II, Leipzig 1897.

AMT   Reginald Campbell Thompson, *Assyrian Medical Texts*, London, 1923.

BAM   Franz Köcher, *Die babylonisch-assyrische Medizin in Texten und Untersuchungen*. Band I: Keilschrifttexte aus Assur, Berlin, 1963. Band II: Keilschrifttexte aus Assur 2, Berlin, 1963. Band III: Keilschrifttexte aus Assur 3, Berlin, 1964. Band IV: Keilschrifttexte aus Assur 4, Babylon, Nippur, Sippar, Uruk und unbekannter Herkunft, Berlin, 1971. Band V: Keilschrifttexte aus Ninive 1. Berlin, New York 1980.

BMS   Leonard William King, *Babylonian Magic and Sorcery, Being 'The Prayers of the Lifting of the Hand'*, London, 1896.

BRM 4   Albert Tobias Clay, *Epics, Hymns, Omens, and Other Texts*, New Haven, 1923 (Babylonian Records in the Library of J. Pierpont Morgan, 4).

BZ   *Biblische Zeitschrift.*

BZAW   *Beiheft* of *ZAW.*

CBQ   *Catholic Biblical Quarterly.*

CT 17   Reginald Campbell Thompson, *Cuneiform Texts from Babylonian Tablets in the British Museum*, vol. 17, London, 1903.

CT 20   Reginald Campbell Thompson, *Cuneiform Texts from Babylonian Tablets in the British Museum*, vol. 20, London, 1904.

JBL   *Journal of Biblical Literature.*

JCS   *Journal of Cuneiform Studies.*

JRAS   *Journal of the Royal Asiatic Society.*

JSOT   *Journal for the Study of the Old Testament.*

JSS   *Journal of Semitic Studies.*

K   Tablets in the Kouyunjik collection of the British Museum.

KAR   Erich Ebeling, *Keilschrifttexte aus Assur religiösen Inhalts*, Leipzig, 1915–23.

LKA   Erich Ebeling, *Literarische Texte aus Assur*, Berlin, 1953.

PBS 1/2   Henry Frederick Lutz, *Selected Sumerian and Babylonian*

Texts, Philadelphia, 1919 (University of Pennsylvania, the Museum, Publications of the Babylonian Section, 1/2).

STT I   Oliver R. Gurney and Jacob J. Finkelstein, *The Sultantepe Tablets*, I, London, 1957.

STT II   Oliver R. Gurney and Peter Hulin, *The Sultantepe Tablets*, II, London, 1964.

UF   *Ugarit-Forschungen.*

VT   *Vetus Testamentum.*

ZAW   *Zeitschrift für alttestamentliche Wissenschaft.*

Notes

1 Enbilulu is a water god, lord of the springs and underground water, son of Ea; Enbilulu is also a name for Marduk/Asalluhi.
2 Ninkarrak is a healing goddess often mentioned in incantations, but otherwise little is known about her character. In the Neo-Assyrian period, Ninkarrak is a name for Gula and a dog is the animal of Gula and of other healing deities as well.
3 *Ashar* is a stone or mineral frequently used in medical prescriptions, mostly crushed and mixed with oil or fat for a salve, for instance against eye troubles; it is also worn against witchcraft. Since it is compared with *huluhhu*, a bright-coloured primitive glass, *ashar* was probably also a sort of bright, transparent stone.
4 The *gipāru*, here translated 'residence', is the dwelling of the *enu*-priest or the *entu*-priestess and the original meaning was probably 'storehouse'. It was the place of the fertility rite of the 'sacred marriage' which explains the mention here.
5 Ninlil, originally a Sumerian goddess and spouse of Enlil, the highest god of the Sumerian pantheon, is in the Neo-Assyrian period, like Ištar, the consort of Aššur.
6 Ningišzidda, also a Sumerian god, belongs to the Nether World where he is guarding the evil demons.
7 Apples and pomegranates are connected with sexuality and love. Pomegranates of gold, carnelian or other precious stones seem to have been popular pieces of jewellery.
8 *tappinnu*-flour is an offering to Ea, the god of fresh water.
9 *mašgašu*: the exact type of this tool or weapon is not known, but perhaps it was a club; it is also the name of a part of a chariot.

10 The Enki gods and Ninki gods are the first generations of gods, the fathers and mothers of the great gods An and Enlil.

11 Eridu, in the extreme south of Babylonia, was the city of Enki.

12 Evil *udug, ala, labasu, asakku* are names of evil demons causing diseases of various kinds. *Lamaštu* was a female demon afflicting babies and pregnant women. The good *udug* (male) and *lamma* (female) were benevolent spirits protecting man against the evil demons.

13 'Ea has done, Ea has undone' is the first line of an often-used incantation.

Bibliography

Abusch, T. (1974) 'Mesopotamian Anti-Witchcraft Literature: Texts and Studies. Part I: The Nature of *Maqlû*: Its Character, Divisions, and Calendrical Setting', *Journal of Near Eastern Studies*, 33: 251–62.

— (1987) *Babylonian Witchcraft Literature: Case Studies* (Atlanta) (Brown Judaic Studies, 132).

— (1989) 'Maqlû' in Dietz Otto Edzard *et al.* eds, *Reallexikon der Assyriologie und Vorderasiatischen Archäologie* (Berlin and New York), 7: 346–51.

— (1990) 'An Early Form of the Witchcraft Ritual *Maqlû* and the Origin of a Babylonian Magical Ceremony' in Tzvi Abusch, John Huehnergard and Piotr Steinkeller eds, *Lingering over Words. Studies in Ancient Near Eastern Literature in Honor of William L. Moran* (Atlanta) (Harvard Semitic Studies, 37): 1–67.

Baudissen, W. W. (1889) *Die Geschichte des Alttestamentlichen Priestertums* (Leipzig).

Beard, M. and North, J. (1990) *Pagan Priests. Religion and Power. in the Ancient World* (London).

Begrich, J. (1934) 'Das priesterliche Hellsorakel', *ZAW*, 52: 81–92.

Berlin, A. (1979) *Enmerkar and Ensuhkešdanna. A Sumerian Narrative Poem* (Philadelphia) (Occasional Publications of the Babylonian Fund, 2).

Biç, M. (1951) 'Der Prophet Amos – ein Hepatoskopos?' *VT*, 1: 293–6.

Biggs, R. D. (1967) *ŠÀ.ZI.GA, Ancient Mesopotamian Potency Incantations* (Locust Valley, New York) (Texts from Cuneiform Sources, 2).

Blau, L. (1898) *Das altjüdische Zauberwesen* (Budapest).

Bottéro, J. (1984) 'Les morts et l'au-delà dans les rituels en accadien contre l'action des "revenants"', *Zeitschrift für Assyriologie* (Berlin), 73: 153–203.

Bryce, G. E. (1975) 'Omen Wisdom in Ancient Israel', *JBL*, 94: 19–37.

Burstein, S. M. (1978) *The* Babyloniaca *of Berossus* (Malibu) (Sources and Monographs, Sources from the Ancient Near East, vol. 1, fascicle 3).

Caplice, R. I. (1965) 'Namburbi Texts in the British Museum I', *Orientalia* NS, 34: 105–31.

— (1967) 'Namburbi Texts in the British Museum III', *Orientalia* NS, 36: 273–98.

— (1970) 'Namburbi Texts in the British Museum IV', *Orientalia* NS, 39: 111–50.

— (1974) *The Akkadian Namburbi Texts: An Introduction* (Los Angeles) (Sources and Monographs, Sources from the Ancient Near East, vol. 1, fascicle 1).

Caquot, A. and Lelbovici, M., eds (1968) *La Divination* (Paris).

Castellino, G. (1955) 'Rituals and Prayers against "Appearing Ghosts"', *Orientalia* NS, 24: 240–74.

Centre d'Etudes Supérieures Spécialisés, ed. (1966) *La divination en Mesopotamie ancienne et dans les régions voisines* (= XIV:e Rencontre Assyriologique Internationale) (Paris).

Coote, R. and Whitelam, K. (1987) *The Emergence of Early Israel in Historical Perspective* (Sheffield).

Cryer, F. H. (1991) 'Der Prophet und der Magier. Bemerkungen anhand einer überholten Diskussion' in Liwak, R. and Wagner, S. eds, *Prophethe und geschichtliche Wirklichkelt im alten Israel* (Stuttgart).

— (1994) *Divination in Ancient Israel and its Near Eastern Environment. A Socio-historical Investigation* (Sheffield).

Davies, P. R. (1995) 'In Search of Ancient Israel', *JSOT*, Sup 148 (Sheffield).

Davies, T. Witton (1898) *Magic, Divination and Demonology Among the Hebrews and their Neighbours* (London and Leipzig).

Daxelmüller C. and Thomsen M.-L. (1982) 'Bildzauber im alten Mesopotamien', *Anthropos. International Review of Ethnology and Lingustics* 77: 27–64.

Delekat, L. (1967) *Asyle und Schutzorakel am Zionheiligtum. Eine Untersuchung zu den privaten Feindpsalmen* (Leiden).

van Dijk, J. (1987) 'Fremdsprachige Beschwörungstexte in der südmesopotamischen literarischen Überlieferung' in Hans Jörg Nissen and Johannes Renger eds, *Mesopotamien und seine Nachbarn. Politische und kulturelle Wechselbeziehungen im alten Vorderasien vom 4 bis 1. Jahrtausend v. Chr.*, 2. verbesserte Auflage (Berlin) (Berliner Beiträge zum Vorderen Orient, 1): 97–110.

Driver G. R. and Miles J. C. (1935) *The Assyrian Laws, Edited with Translation and Commentary* (Oxford reprint: Darmstadt, 1975).

— (1952) *The Babylonian Laws I, Legal Commentary* (Oxford).

— (1955) *The Babylonian Laws II, Transliterated Text, Translation, Philological Notes, Glossary* (Oxford).

Ebach, J. and Rilterswijrden, U. (1977, 1980) 'Unterweltsbeschwörung im Alten Testament', *UF*, 9: 57–70; *UF*, 12: 205–20.

Ebeling, E. (1931a) 'Aus dem Tagewerk eines assyrischen Zauberpriesters', *Mitteilungen der Altorientalischen Gesellschaft*, 5/3: 3–52.

— (1931b) *Tod und Leben nach den Vorstellungen der Babylonier* (Berlin, Leipzig).

— (1953) *Die akkadische Gebetsserie 'Handerhebung' von neuem gesammelt und herausgegeben* (Berlin).

— (1954) 'Beiträge zur Kenntnis der Beschwörungsserie Namburbi', *Revue d'assyriologie et d'archéologie orientale*, 48:178–91.

— (1955a) 'Ein neuassyrisches Beschwörungsritual gegen Bann und Tod', *Zeitschrift für Assyriologie*, 51 (neue Folge 17): 167–79.

— (1955b) 'Beiträge zur Kenntnis der Beschwörungsserie Namburbi', *Revue d'assyriologie et d'archéologie orientale*, 49: 178–92.

Edzard, D. O. (1987) 'Literatur', in D. O. Edzard ed., *Reallexikon der Assyriologie und vorderasiatischen Archäologie* (Berlin, New York), 7: 35–48.

Ehrlich, E. L. (1953) *Der Traum im Alten Testament* (Berlin).

Evans-Pritchard, E. E. (1937) *Witchcraft, Oracles and Magic among the Azande* (Oxford).

Falkenstein, A. (1931) *Die Haupttypen der sumerischen Beschwörung literarisch untersucht,* (Leipzig) (Leipziger Semitistische Studien, neue Folge 1). Reprint Leipzig 1968.

— (1964) 'Ein sumerischer Liebeszauber', *Zeitschrift für Assyriologie,* 56: 113–29.

— (1966) ' "Wahrsagung" in der sumerischen Überleiferung' in *La divination en Mésopotamie ancienne et dans les régions voisines. XIVe Rencontre Assyriologique Internationale* (*Strasbourg, 2–6 juillet 1965*), (Paris) (Travaux du Centre d'études supérieures specialisé d'histoire des religions de Strasbourg): 45–68.

Falkenstein A. and von Soden, W. (1953) *Sumerische und akkadische Hymnen und Gebete* (Zürich, Stuttgart).

Farber W. (1977) *Beschwörungsrituale an Ištar und Dumuzi. Attī Ištar ša harmaša Dumuzi* (Wiesbaden) (Akademie der Wissenschaften und der Literatur, Veröffentlichungen der orientalischen Kommission, 30).

— (1981) 'Zur älteren akkadischen Beschwörungsliteratur', *Zeitschrift für Assyriologie,* 71: 51–72.

— (1983) 'Lamaštu' in Dietz Otto Edzard ed., *Reallexikon der Assyriologie und vorderasiatischen Archäologie* (Berlin, New York) 6: 439–46.

—(1987) 'Tamarisken – Fibeln – Skolopender. Zur philologischen Deutung der "Reiseszene" auf neuassyrischen Lamaštu–Amuletten' in Francesca Rochberg-Halton, ed., *Language, Literature, and History: Philological and Historical Studies Presented to Erica Reiner* (New Haven) (American Oriental Series, 67): 85–105.

— (1989) *Schlaf, Kindchen, Schlaf! Mesopotamische Baby-Beschwörungen und – Rituale* (Winona Lake) (Mesopotamian Civilizations, 2).

Finkel, I. L. (1983–4) 'Necromancy in Ancient Mesopotamia', *Archiv für Orientforschung*, 29–30: 1–17.

— (1988) 'Adad-apla-iddina, Esagil-kīn-apli, and the Series SA.GIG' in Erle Leichty, Maria deJong Ellis and Pamela Gerardi, eds, *A Scientific Humanist. Studies in Memory of Abraham Sachs* (Philadelphia) (Occasional Publications of the Samuel Noah Kramer Fund, 9): 143–59.

Fox, R. L. (1988) *Pagans and Christians in the Mediterranean World from the Second Century AD to the Conversion of Constantine* (London).

Frymer-Kensky, T. S. (1977) 'The Judicial Ordeal in the Ancient Near East', PhD dissertation, Yale University.

Garbini, G. (1986) *Storia e ideologies nell'Israele antico* (Brescia).

— (1997) *Gli filistei* (Brescia).

Geller, M. J. (1980) 'The *Šhurpu* Incantations and Lev. V.1–5', *JSS*, 25: 181–92.

— (1985) *Forerunners to Udug-hul, Sumerian Exorcistic Incantations* (Stuttgart) (Freiburger altorientalische Studien, 12).

Gnuse, R. (1982) 'A Reconsideration of the Form-Critical Structure in 1 Samuel 3: An Ancient Near Eastern Dream Theophany', *ZAW*, 94: 379–90.

— (1984) *The Dream Theophany of Samuel: Its Structure in Relation to Ancient Near Eastern Dreams and its Theological Significance* (Lanham, Maryland).

Goody, J. (1968) *Literacy in Traditional Societies* (Cambridge).

— (1977) *The Domestication of the Savage Mind* (Cambridge).

— (1990) *The Oriental, the Ancient and the Primitive. Systems of Marriage and the Family in the Pre-industrial Societies of Eurasia* (Cambridge).

Grayson, A. K. (1975) *Assyrian and Babylonian Chronicles* (Locust Valley, New York) (Texts from Cuneiform Sources, 5).

Guillaume, A. (1938) *Prophecy and Divination* (London).

Haas, V. (1980) 'Die Dämonisierung des Fremden und des Feindes im Alten Orient', *Rocznik Orientalistyczny*, 41/2: 37–44.

Hopkins, D. C. (1985) *The Highlands of Canaan: Agricultural Life in the Early Iron Age* (Sheffield).

Haldar, A. (1945) *Associations of Cult Prophets among the Ancient Semites* (Uppsala).

Horowitz, W. (1992) 'Two Abnu šikinšu Fragments and Related Matters', *Zeitschrift für Assyriologie*, 32: 112–22.

Jamieson-Drake, D. (1991) *Scribes and Schools in Monarchic Judah: A Socio-Archaeological Approach* (Sheffield).

Jeffers, A. (1996) *Magic and Divination in Ancient Palestine and Syria* (Leiden).

Jeyes, U. (1989) *Old Babylonian Extispicy. Omen Texts in the British Museum* (Istanbul, Leiden) (Uitgaven van het Nederlands historisch-archaeologisch Instituut te Istanbul, 64).

Jirku, A. (1913) 'Mantik in Altisrael'. Inaugural Dissertation (Rostock).

—— (1961) 'Zu den altisraelitischen Vorstellungen von Toten- und Ahnengeistern', *BZ*, 5: 30–8.

Johnson, A. R. (1944) *The Cultic Prophet in Ancient Israel* (Cardiff).

Kieckhefer, R. (1976) *European Witch Trials: Their Foundations in Popular and Learned Culture 1300–1500* (London).

—— (1989) *Magic in the Middle Ages* (Cambridge).

Knauf, E.-A (Belleri) (1995) *Die Umwelt des Alten Testaments* (Stuttgart).

Kilchler, F. (1917) 'Das priesterliche Orakel in Israel und Judaea' in Frankenberg, W. and Kilchler, F. eds, *ZAW*, Beiheft 33.

Köcher, F. (1966) 'Die Ritualtafel der magisch-medizinischen Tafelserie "Einreibung"', *Archiv für Orientforschung*, 21: 13–20.

—— (1980) *Die babylonisch-assyrische Medizin in Texten und Untersuchungen. Band V: Keilschrifttexte aus Ninive 1* (Berlin, New York).

Krebernik, M. (1984) *Die Beschwörungen aus Fara und Ebla* (Hildesheim) (Texte und Studien zur Orientalistik, 2).

Kuhn, P. (1989) *Offenbarungsstimmen im Antiken Judentum. Unter-*

suchungen zur bat qol und verwandten Phänomenen. Texte und Studien zum antiken Judentum, 20 (Tübingen).

Kümmel, H. M. (1968) 'Ersatzkönig und Sündenbock' in *ZAW*, 80: 289–318.

Labat, R. (1951) *Traité akkadien de diagnostics et prognostics médicaux* (Leiden).

— (1965) *Un calendrier babylonien des travaux des signes et des mois* (*séries iqqur îpuš*). (Paris) (Bibliothèque de l'École des Hautes Études, IVᵉ section (sciences historiques et philologiques), 321).

— (1975) 'Hemerologien' in D. O. Edzard ed., *Reallexikon der Assyriologie und vorderasiatischen Archäologie* (Berlin, New York), 4: 317–23.

Lambert, W. G. (1957–8) 'An Incantation of the Maqlû Type', *Archiv für Orientforschung*, 18: 288–99.

— (1960*) Babylonian Wisdom Literature* (Oxford).

Leichty, E. (1970) *The Omen Series Šumma Izbu* (Locust Valley, New York) (Texts from Cuneiform Sources, 4).

Lemche, N. P. (1985) *Early Israel. Anthropological and Historical Studies on the Israelite Society Before the Monarchy* (Leiden).

— (1991) *The Canaanites and Their Land* (Sheffield).

— (1996) *Die Vorgeschichte Israels. Von den Anfangen bis zum Ausgang des 13. Jahrhunderts v. Chr.* (Stuttgart).

Lenormant, F. (1875) *Choix de textes cunéiformes inédits ou incomplétement publiés* (Paris).

Lewis, I. M. (1971) *Ecstatic Religion* (Harmondsworth).

— (1976) *Social Anthropology in Perspective* (Harmondsworth).

— (1986) *Religion in Context: Cults and Charisma* (Cambridge).

Lindblom, Johs. (1962) *Prophecy in Ancient Israel* (Oxford).

— (1962b) 'Lot-casting in the Old Testament', *VT*, 12: 164–78.

Long, B. O. (1973) 'The Effect of Divination Upon Israelite Literature', *JBL*, 92: 489–97.

Lust, J. (1974) 'On Wizards and Prophets', *VT*, 26: 133–42.

McKay, J. (1973) *Religion in Judah under the Assyrians* (London).

Maler, J. (1965) *Das Altisraelitische Ladeheiligtum* (Berlin).

— (1969) 'Urim und Thummim', *Kairos* 11: 22–38.

Mauss, M. and Hubert, H. (1902–3) 'Esquisse d'une théorie sociale de la magie', *L'année sociologique*.

Mayer, W. (1976) *Untersuchungen zur Formensprache der babylonischen 'Gebetsbeschwörungen'* (Rome) (Studia Pohl, Series maior, 5).

Meier, G. (1937) *Die assyrische Beschwörungssammlung Maqlû* (Berlin) (*Archiv für Orientforschung*, Beiheft 2).

Michalowski, P. (1985) 'On Some Early Sumerian Magical Texts', *Orientalia* NS, 54: 216–25.

Mowinckel, S. (1921) *Psalmenstudien I. Åwän und die individuellen Klagepsalmen* (Kristiania).

— (1923) *Psalmenstudien III. Die Kultprophete und prophetische Psalmen* (Kristiania).

Murtonen, A. (1952) 'The Prophet Amos – A Hepatoscoper?' *VT*, 2: 170–1.

O'Keefe, D. L. (1982) *Stolen Lightning. The Social Theory of Magic* (Oxford).

Oppenheim, A. L. (1956) *The Interpretation of Dreams in the Ancient Near East. With a Translation of an Assyrian Dream-Book* (Philadelphia) (*Transactions of the American Philosophical Society*, NS, vol. 46, part 3: 177–373).

— (1964) *Ancient Mesopotamia. Portrait of a Dead Civilization* (Chicago).

Park, G. K. (1963) 'Divination and its Social Contexts', *JRAS*, 93: 195–209.

Parpola, S. (1970) *Letters from Assyrian Scholars to the Kings Esarhaddon and Assurbanipal. Part I: Texts* (Kevelaer, Neukirchen-Vluyn) (Alter Orient und Altes Testament, 5/1).

— (1983) *Letters from Assyrian Scholars to the Kings Esarhaddon and Assurbanipal. Part II: Commentary and Appendices* (Kevelaer, Neukirchen-Vluyn) (Alter Orient und Altes Testament. 5/2).

Pettinato, G. (1966) *Die Ölwahrsagung bei den Babyloniern, I: Einleitung, II: Texte und Kommentar* (Rome) (Studi Semitici, 21–2).

Pingree, D. 'Mesopotamian Astronomy and Astral Omens in Other Civilizations' in Nissen, H. J. and Renger, J. eds, *Mesopotamian und seine Nachbarn*, 2: 613–31.

Porter, P. A. (1983) *Metaphors and Monsters. A Literary-Critical Study of Daniel 7 and 8* (Uppsala).

Pritchard, J.B, ed. (1958) *The Ancient Near East, vol I. An Anthology of Texts and Pictures* (Princeton).

Reiner, E. (1958) *Šurpu, a Collection of Sumerian and Akkadian Incantations* (Graz) (*Archiv für Orientforschung*, Beiheft 11).

— (1960a) 'Fortune-Telling in Mesopotamia', *Journal of Near Eastern Studies*, 19: 23–35.

— (1960b) 'Plaque Amulets and House Blessings', *Journal of Near Eastern Studies*, 19: 148–55.

— (1985) 'The Uses of Astrology', *Journal of the American Oriental Society*, 105: 589–95.

— (1990) 'Nocturnal Talk' in Tzvi Abusch, John Huehnergard and Piotr Steinkeller eds, *Lingering over Words. Studies in Ancient Near Eastern Literature in Honor of William L. Moran* (Atlanta) (Harvard Semitic Studies, 37): 421–4.

Richter, W. (1963) 'Traum und Traumdeutung im AT. Ihre Form und Verwendung', *BZ* (NF), 7: 202–20.

Ricks, S. D. (1995) 'The Magician as Outsider in the Hebrew Bible and the New Testament' in Meyer, M. and Mirecki, P. eds, *Ancient Magic and Ritual Power* (Leiden): 131–43.

Ritter, E. K. (1965) 'Magical-expert (= *āšipu*) and Physician (= *asû*): Notes on Two Complementary Professions in Babylonian Medicine' in *Studies in Honor of Benno Landsberger on his Seventy-Fifth Birthday April 21, 1965* (Chicago) (Assyriological Studies, 16): 299–321.

Roberts, J. J. M. (1977) 'Of Signs, Prophets, and Time Limits: A Note on Psalm 74: 9–11', *CBQ*, 39: 474–81.

Rochberg-Halton, F. (1984) 'Canonicity in Cuneiform Texts', *Journal of Cuneiform Studies*, 36: 127–44.

— (1988) *Aspects of Babylonian Celestial Divination. The Lunar Eclipse Tablets of Enuma Anu Enlil* (Horn, Austria) (*Archiv für Orientforschung* Beiheft, 22).

Röllig, W. (1987) 'Literatur' in D. O. Edzard ed., *Rallexikon der Assyriologie und vorderasiatischen Archäologie* (Berlin, New York), 7: 48–66.

Rollin, S. (1983) 'Women and Witchcraft in Ancient Assyria (*c.* 900–600 BC)' in Averil Cameron and Amélie Kuhrt eds, *Images of Women in Antiquity* (London and Canberra): 34–45.

Saggs, H. W. F. (1978) *The Encounter with the Divine in Mesopotamia and Israel* (London).

Schmidt, B. B. (1995) 'The "Witch" of En-Dor, 1 Sam 28, and Ancient Near Eastern Necromancy' in Meyer, M. and Mirecki, P. eds, *Ancient Magic and Ritual Power* (Leiden): 111–29.

Schmidtke, F. (1967) 'Träume, Orakel und Totengeister als Kinder der Zukunft in Babylonien', *BZ*, 11: 240–46.

Spencer, J. (1670) *Dissertatio de Urim et Thummim in Deuteron. c.33.v.8 In qua Eorum natura et origo Non paucorum rituum Mos & eorum rationes, et Obscuriora quaedam Scripturae loca probabiliter explicantur* (Cambridge).

Spleckermann, H. (1982) *Juda unter Assur in der Sargonidenzeit* (Göttingen).

Starr, I. (1983) *The Rituals of the Diviner* (Malibu) (*Bibliotheca Mesopotamica*, 12).

Thierseh, H. (1936) *Ependytes und Ephod. Gottesbild und Priesterkleid im alten Vorderasien* (Stuttgart).

Thomas, K. (1973) *Religion and the Decline of Magic* (London).

Thompson, R. C. (1900) *The Reports of the Magicians and Astrologers of Nineveh and Babylon. I: The Cuneiform Texts; II: English Translations, Vocabulary* (London).

— (1903) *The Devils and Evil Spirits of Babylonia, vol. I: 'Evil Spirits'* (London).

— (1904) *The Devils and Evil Spirits of Babylonia, vol. II: 'Fever Sickness' and 'Headache'* (London).

— (1930) 'Assyrian Prescriptions for Treating Bruises or Swellings', *The American Journal of Semitic Languages and Literatures*, 47: 1–25.

Thompson, T. L. (1992) *Early History of the Israelite People. From the Written and Archaeological Sources* (Leiden).

Thomsen, M.-L. (1983) 'Die Vorläufer der abendländischen Magie' in *Kindlers Enzyklopädie: Der Mensch 4* (Zürich): 688–90.

— (1987) *Zauberdiagnose und Schwarze Magie in Mesopotamien* (Copenhagen) (CNI Publications, 2).

— (1988) 'The Wisdom of the Chaldaeans. Mesopotamian Magic as Conceived by Classical Authors' in Tobias Fischer-Hansen ed., *Cultural Influences Between East and West in the Ancient World* (Copenhagen) (Acta Hyperborea, 1): 93–101.

— (1992) 'The Evil Eye in Mesopotamia', *Journal of the Near Eastern Society*, 51: 19–32.

Toorn, K. van der (1988) 'Echoes of Judaean Necromancy in Isaiah 28, 7–22', *ZAW*, 100: 199–217.

Trevor-Roper, H. R. (1969) *The European Witch-Craze of the Sixteenth and Seventeenth Centuries* (Harmondsworth).

Tropper, J. (1989) *Nekromantie. Totenbefragung im Alten Orient und im Alten Testament* (Kevelaer, Neukirchen-Vluyn) (Alter Orient und Altes Testament, 223).

Tsukimoto, A. (1985) *Untersuchungen zur Totenpflege* (kispum) *im alten Mesopotamien* (Kevelaer, Neukirchen-Vluyn) (Alter Orient und Altes Testament, 216).

Turner, V. (1967) *The Forest of Symbols. Aspects of Ndembu Ritual* (Ithaca).

Ulmer, R. (1994) *The Evil Eye in the Bible and Rabbinic Literature* (Hoboken, NJ).

Ungnad, A. (1941–4) 'Besprechungskunst und Astrologie in Babylonien', *Archiv für Orientforschung*, 14: 251–84.

Ussishkin, D. and Woodhead, I. (1992) 'Excavations at Tel Jezreel 1990–1991. Preliminary Report', *Tel Aviv*, 19: 3–56.

— (1994) '1992–1993. Second Preliminary Report', *Levant*, 26: 1–48.

— (1997) '1994–1996. Third Preliminary Report', *Tel Aviv*, 24: 6–72.

van der Waerden, B. L. (1980) *Erwachende Wissenschaft. Band 2: Die Anfänge der Astronomie*. (2. Auflage Basel, Boston, Stuttgart) (Wissenschaft und Kultur, 23).

Walters, S. D. (1970) 'The Sorceress and Her Apprentice. A Case Study of an Accusation', *JCS*, 23: 27–38.

von Weiher, E. (1981) 'Bemerkungen zu § 2 KH und zur Anwendung des Flußordals', *Zeitschrift für Assyriologie*, 71: 95–102.

— (1983) *Spätbabylonische Texte aus Uruk*. Teil II (Berlin) (Ausgrabungen der deutschen Forschungsgemeinschaft in Uruk-Warka, 10).

Westenholz, J. and A. (1977) 'Help for Rejected Suitors. The Old Akkadian Love Incantation MAD V 8', *Orientalia* NS, 46: 198–219.

Whitelam, K. W. (1996) *The Invention of Ancient Israel. The Silencing of Palestinian History* (London).

Wilson, B. R. (1970) *Rationality* (Oxford).

Wilson, R. R. (1980) *Prophecy and Society in Ancient Israel* (Philadelphia).

Wright, J. (1975) 'Did Amos Inspect Livers?', *Australian Biblical Review*, 23.

Yamauchi, E. M. (1967) *Mandaic Incantation Bowls* (New Haven).

Zimmern, H. (1915–16) 'Zu den "Keilschrifttexten aus Assur religiösen Inhalts"', *Zeitschrift für Assyriologie*, 30: 184–213.

Index